Planting Seeds of Faith

A Companion Volume to Walking the Path of Faith

Planting Seeds of Faith

Fun Character-building Activities for LDS Children

A Companion Volume to

Walking the Path of Faith

Alison Palmer

Second Printing: July, 2004

International Standard Book Number
0-88290-763-8

Horizon Publishers' Catalog and Order Number
H2105

Printed and distributed
in the United States of America by

CEDAR FORT

Address:
925 North Main Street
Springville, Utah 84663

Phone:
Local Phone: (801) 489-4084
WATS (toll free): 1 (800) SKYBOOK
FAX: (800) 489-1097

Internet:
Website: http://www.horizonpublishersbooks.com

Acknowledgments

The Author wishes to thank Jennifer Beckett and George Hemingway for their hard work creating the illustrations included in this book.

Appreciation also is expressed to Duane and Jean Crowther, senior editors at Horizon Publishers, and to Sam Richardson and Jenny Beckstead, who typeset and proof-read the book.

Table of Contents

MY GOSPEL STANDARDS

I will follow Heavenly Father's plan for me.
I will remember my baptismal covenant and listen to the Holy Ghost.
I will choose the right. I know I can repent when I make a mistake.
I will be honest with Heavenly Father, others, and myself.
I will use the names of Heavenly Father and Jesus Christ reverently. I will not swear or use crude words.
I will do those things on the Sabbath that will help me feel close to Heavenly Father and Jesus Christ.
I will honor my parents and do my part to strengthen my family.
I will keep my mind and body sacred and pure, and I will not partake of things that are harmful to me.
I will dress modestly to show respect for Heavenly Father and myself.
I will only read and watch things that are pleasing to Heavenly Father.
I will only listen to music that is pleasing to Heavenly Father.
I will seek good friends and treat others kindly.
I will live now to be worthy to go to the temple, serve a mission, and do my part to have an eternal family.

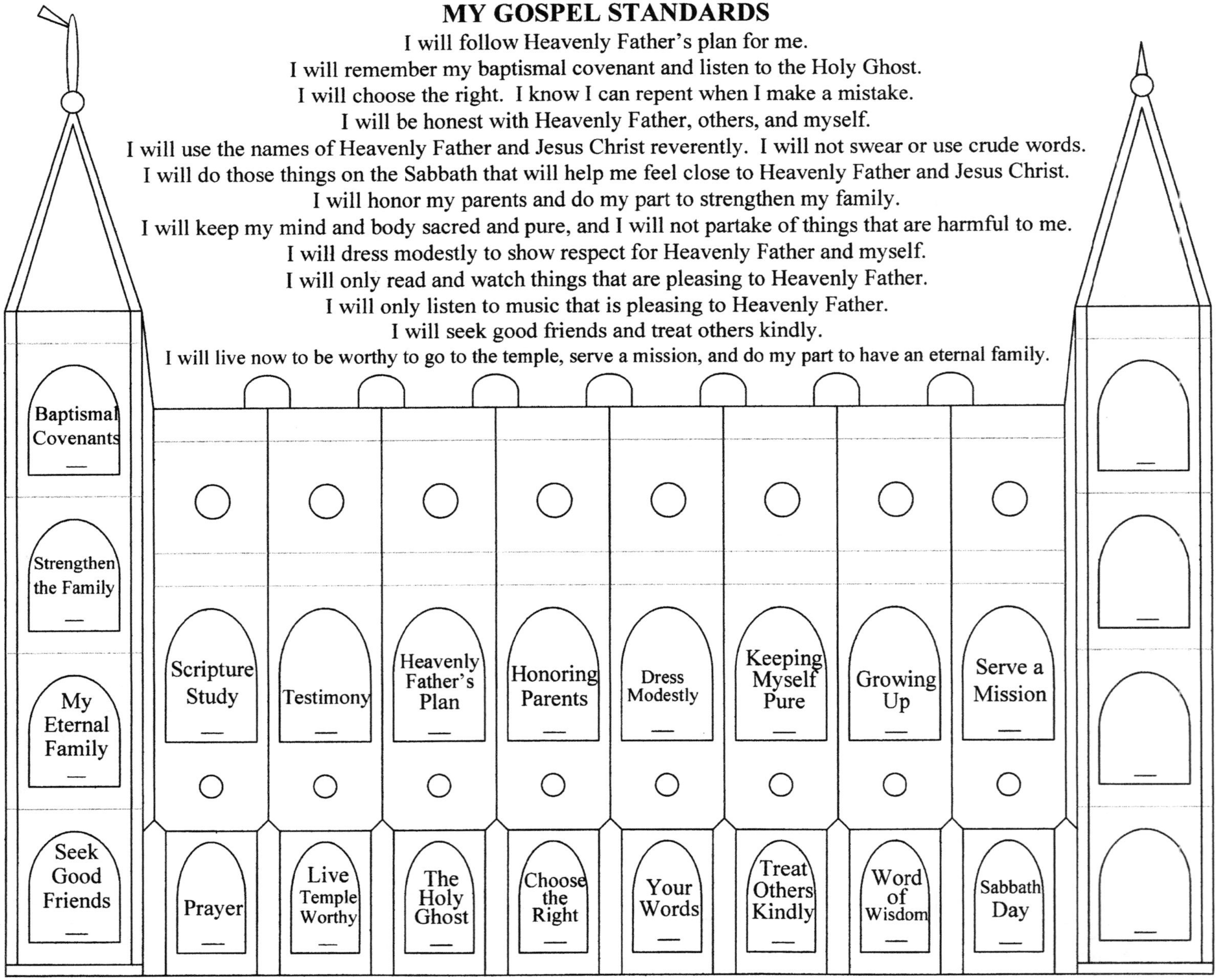

- The outer picture lists the basic themes to be covered and allows a place to number them for order of coverage during the year.
- The inside windows give the title of a corresponding lesson from this book and a place to list the date it was taught.
- Blank windows are included for customization.
- You may also may a copy of the diagram, block out the words and re-copy it allowing you to completely customize your calendar.

Instructions:

- Copy both pages onto cardstock paper.
- Color the outer picture and number the topics in order to be covered.
- Use a hobby knife to cut the 24 windows on their curved lines only, leave the flat lines intact.
- Place the temple picture on top of lesson sheet and verify placement before gluing in place.

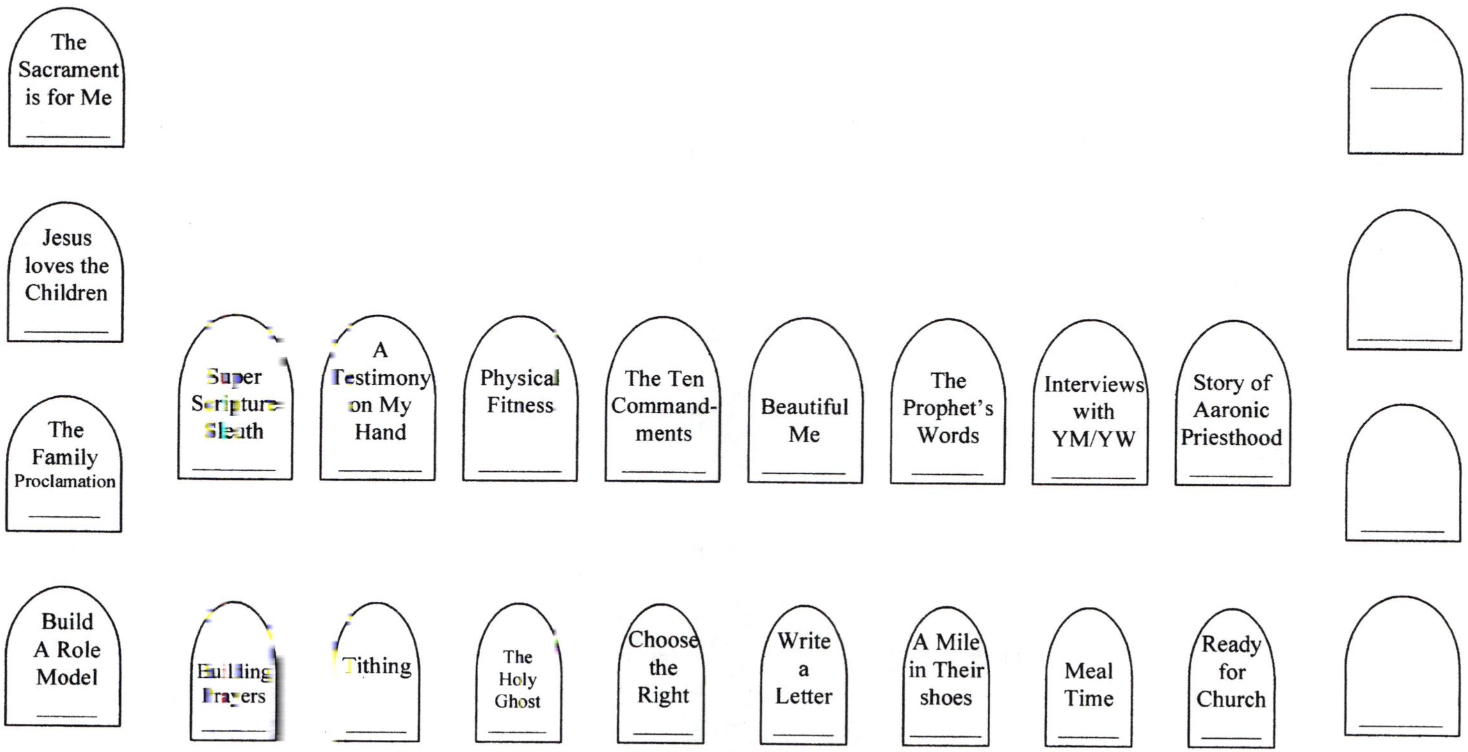

One
A Mile in Their Shoes

Scripture: "Thus speaketh the Lord of hosts, saying, Execute true judgment, and shew mercy and compassions every man to his brother."

—Zechariah 7:9

Song: "I'll Walk with You," *Children's Songbook*, pg. 140.

Treat: Foot shaped cookies or shoestring potato sticks

Lesson:
Materials Needed:
* Chalkboard and chalk
* Books from the library on children with disabilities

This would be an appropriate time to invite someone that you know who has a disability, or a child with a disability, to visit your group and talk with them about what they have learned about their disability. Have them express ways children can be respectful and helpful to those with disabilities.

If you are unable to find a guest speaker, be prepared to hold the activity first, then allow the children to discuss their experiences and list their own ideas for appropriate behavior. Provide a look at several disabilities by visiting your local library for storybooks on children with disabilities. Suggestions are noted here, all stories listed are in picture book format for ease of sharing in a group situation. You may wish to have your librarian suggest some age appropriate books for independent reading.

* *See the Ocean* by Estella Condra
* *Arnie and the New Kid* by Nancy L. Carlson
* *Special People, Special Ways* by Arlene Maguire
* *Extraordinary Friends (Let's Talk About It)* by Fred Rogers
* *Someone Special, Just Like You* (An Owlet Book) by Tricia Brown
* *Howie helps Himself* by Joan Fassler
* *My Sister Is Special* by Larry Jansen, et al
* *Lee, the Rabbit with Epilepsy* (Special Needs Collection) by Deborah M. Moss
* *Taking Cerebral Palsy to School* by Mary Elizabeth Anderson
* *Rolling Along: The Story of Taylor and His Wheelchair* by Jamee Riggio Heelan
* *Ben, King of the River* by David Gifaldi
* *Princess Pooh* by Kathleen M. Muldoon, et al

* *My Brother Sammy* by Becky Edwards
* *Earl the EMU God Has a Purpose for Those Who Are Different* by Pat Winston
* *Rainbow Joe and Me* by Maria Diaz Strom

Activity:

Materials Needed:

* Wheelchair if available in your unit, or substitute a child's wagon
* Two sets of earplugs or earmuffs
* Several blindfolds
* 2 towels or fabric that can be used to bind a child's arm to his side, use the other one to bind both of another child's arms

Randomly assign the children to a disability and task to be accomplished within a set amount of time (approximately five minutes). Rotate several times so that each child gets to experience several different things.

* The wheelchair-restricted child must push themselves around the parameter of the church or house.
* Two children in earmuffs must play a game of charades and guess what each other needs without using words of any kind. (i.e.—I need a drink of water, My nose tickles, Shake my hand please) You might want to allow them paper and pencil or the chalkboard to help them write down their guesses at the charades since they can't speak in return.
* The children in blindfolds must successfully navigate the room or other area.
* The child with only one arm must put on his coat or serve himself refreshments unassisted.
* The child with both arms restricted must find a way to write his name.

Special note: Some disabilities are not quite as obvious as these are. You might want to be sensitive to those with learning disabilities by doing some of the following.

* Not allowing a child to interact with the other children—autism.
* Give a child a book written in a foreign language and asking them to tell you what it says—dyslexia or learning disabilities.

If there is a specific need within your ward, this is your opportunity to do so in a non-threatening way.

Use this lesson to reinforce:

* *My Gospel Standards*
* *Faith in God*, for boys and girls, serving others
* *Family Home Evening Resource Book*, lesson 24
* *Primary 1*, lessons 16 through 22 and 34
* *Aaronic Priesthood 2*, lesson 50
* *Young Women 2*, lesson 49
* *New Testament Gospel Doctrine Manual*, lesson 12

Two
Meal Time

Scripture: "Yea, and the herb, and the good things which come of the earth, whether for food or for raiment, or for houses, or for barns, or for orchards, or for gardens, or for vineyards; Yea, all things which come of the earth, in the season thereof, are made for the benefit and the use of man, both to please the eye and to gladden the heart; Yea, for food and for raiment, for taste and for smell, to strengthen the body and to enliven the soul."

—D&C 59:17-19

Song: "Thanks to Our Father," *Children's Songbook*, pg. 20.

Treat: Granola bars and milk or other healthy snack

Lesson:

Materials Needed:

* Color, cut and laminate the refrigerator and foods included in this lesson
* Sandwich bag, tape this to the back of the refrigerator to hold the foods
* Diagram of the food pyramid
* Paper and pencil for each child

Show the children the picture of the food pyramid and explain to them that this is a way to try and make sure that they are eating things that are healthy for them and eating them in the right amounts. Ask them to name some of their favorite foods and show them where they would fit into the food pyramid. Show them what kinds of foods are included on each level and the amounts that should be eaten.

Show the children the refrigerator. Ask each child to take turns coming up and drawing a food out of the bag. As each food is drawn help the children decide if it is a good choice or bad food choice.

Remind the children that what we eat is a big factor in keeping the bodies Heavenly Father has given us healthy. Allow them to voice other things that they can do.

Ask each child to write down everything that they have eaten that day. Then help them separate the foods into categories and servings. How have they done eating a well balanced diet? Encourage them to continue writing down everything they eat during the coming week. How can they make better choices, where are they already making good choices?

Activity:

Materials Needed:

* Old grocery store sales ads
* Masking tape
* Scissors
* Large clear area to work in

Before the meeting, use the tape to construct a large food pyramid on the floor.

Have the children cut out pictures of their favorite foods from the sales ads. They should then decide where it should go and place them inside the pyramid. Continue until you have a large variety of foods represented and they are placing them with some accuracy that shows their understanding.

Next divide the children into three groups and assign them a meal (breakfast, lunch or dinner) to "prepare" from the things they have chosen to put in the pyramid. When the groups have all chosen, assemble their day's meals.

Then help them break the meals into servings and see how well balanced their meals were. See if there are substitutions that could be made to make the meals healthier.

Replace the pieces and have the children break into two teams. Run relay races to compose meals. Each player must run to the pyramid and choose one food, then run back and tag the next person to do the same thing. When everyone has chosen a food, the ultimate victory goes to the team whose meal is the best balanced and healthy.

Use this lesson to reinforce:

* *My Gospel Standards*
* *Faith in God*, learning and living the gospel, serving others and developing talents
* Cub Scouts Wolf Achievement 8, Bear Achievement 9 and Webelos "fitness"
* *Family Home Evening Resource Book*, lesson idea "word of wisdom"
* *Primary 3*, lesson 14
* *Primary 5*, lesson 24
* *Primary 6*, lesson 40
* *Aaronic Priesthood 1*, lesson 18
* *Aaronic Priesthood 2*, lesson 27
* *Aaronic Priesthood 3*, lesson 27
* *Young Women 1*, lesson 38
* *D&C and Church History Gospel Doctrine Manual*, lesson 22
* *Gospel Principles*, chapter 29

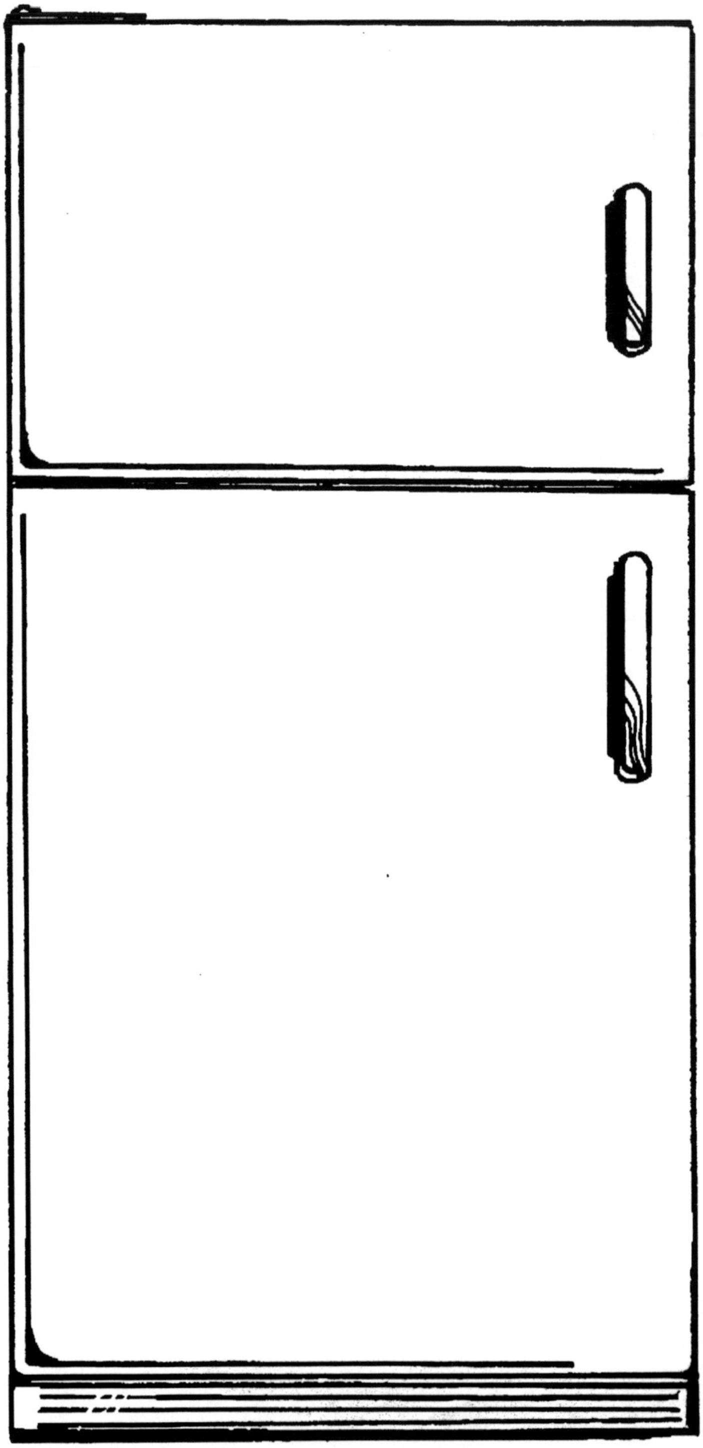

MILK
SODA
EGGS
ICE CREAM
CHIPS
CANDY

Three
"Choose the Right"
Hymn #239

Scripture: "Say unto this people: Choose ye this day, to serve the Lord God who made you. Behold my Spirit is upon you, wherefore all thy words will I justify; and the mountains shall flee before you, and the rivers shall flee before you, and the rivers shall turn from their course; and thou shalt abide in me, and I in you; therefore walk with me."

—Moses 6:33

Song: "I Pledge Myself to Love the Right," *Children's Songbook*, pg. 161.

Treat: Fruit Chews in a bag labeled "I Can Chews the Right"

Lesson:

Materials Needed:

* Hymnals for each child
* Pianist or other form of accompaniment for Hymn #239
* Chalk and chalkboard

Ask the children if any of them have ever been hiking. Let them share their experiences with you. Describe a trip of your own to them. Share a story (either hiking or life experience) where you had something difficult to do such as climbing a hill. Describe how you went about accomplishing the task. Then describe the rewards that came from doing the task even though it was difficult.

Help the children understand that during our lives we will have choices to make that may seem difficult, like hiking up a steep hill. But, when we make the right choice and do our best there can be wonderful rewards, such as a beautiful view from the top of that hill and a feeling of accomplishment and satisfaction. When we learn to choose the right we are learning to see things as Heavenly Father sees them and we are trying to be more like Him. It brings us great happiness that we can't find any other way.

Draw a mountain on the chalkboard while the children look up Hymn #239 in their hymnals. Read through the words of the verses with the children; show them how the words are broken into phrases by punctuation marks. Then, have the children follow the path of the notes on the top staff with their finger and tell you what they notice happening with each phrase. It may be difficult for them to notice at first, so use the mountain you drew to help illustrate that each phrase of the song climbs a small mountain then comes back down.

Sing the first line with the children while they trace a mountain as their voices go up and down. Spend some time with them discovering and tracing each of the mountains, sing the phrases individually while they become accustomed to the rhythm and movement of the song. During this process stop and define any words or phrases that they question.

This song is a promise of Heavenly Father's blessings for choosing His ways instead of the worlds. Discuss the challenges and promises stated in the words and continue to practice singing the phrases. When the children are comfortable with at least the first verse have them stand as they sing the whole song. They can use their bodies to show the motion of the notes by squatting and standing as the notes go up and down.

Close the exercise with your own testimony of the benefits of staying close to the Lord and making good choices.

Activity:

Materials Needed:

* Copies of the choosing maze for each child
* Writing utensils for each child

Tell the children in this maze they will be faced with choices to make. They will go forward until a diversion of the path comes. You will present a situation to them for them to decide upon. If a choice is good then they should turn to the right in the maze. If a choice is bad and should be avoided, they will turn to the left. If they make all the correct choices they will find their way through.

**Note:* It helps to have the children re-orient the maze so that they are always going forward and it is clear which way is right and which is left. The answer key is numbered in order of the situation to be read.

1. You bring a friend to church with you. (right)
2. You cleaned your room without your mother reminding you. (right)
3. You lied about where you were going with your friends after school. (left)
4. You fought with your sister over who got to sit in the front seat. (left)
5. You cheated on a test at school. (left)
6. You bought a CD that had some inappropriate music on it. (left)
7. You paid your tithing Sunday. (right)
8. You say your prayers every night. (right)
9. You made a goal to read your scriptures every day. (right)
10. You tried the cigarette someone offered you. (left)

Use this lesson to reinforce:

* *My Gospel Standards*
* *Faith in God*, learning and living the gospel
* Cub Scouts Wolf, Bear and Webelos religious requirements, also Wolf Achievement 12 and Elective 11d and Bear Achievement 24e
* *Family Home Evening Resource Book*, lesson 8 and lesson idea "music"
* *Primary 2*
* *Primary 3*
* *Gospel Principles*, chapter 4
* *For the Strength of Youth*
* *Aaronic Priesthood 1*, lesson 20

"Choose the Right" Maze

Start

Finish

"Choose the Right" Maze

Answer Key

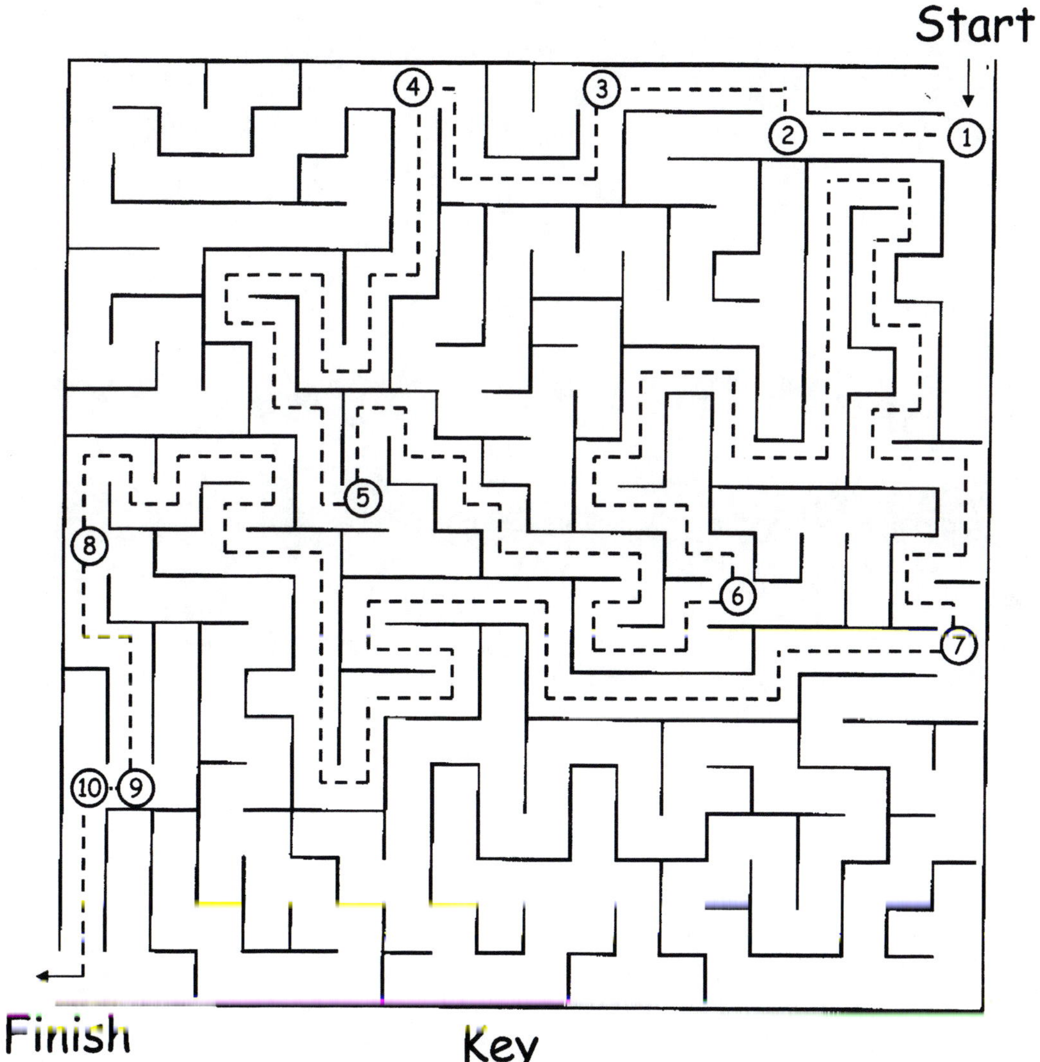

Key

(N)= Decision Point "N"

Four
The Prophet's Words for Me

Scripture: "Wherefore, meaning the church, thou shalt give heed unto all his words and commandments which he shall give unto you as he receiveth them, walking in all holiness before me; For his word ye shall receive, as if from mine own mouth, in all patience and faith."
—D&C 21:4-5

Song: "Stand for the Right," *Children's Songbook*, pg. 159

Treat: Hershey Kisses®

Lesson:
Materials Needed:
* Obtain a copy of President Gordon B. Hinkley's "A Prophet's Counsel and Prayer for Youth", Ensign, Jan. 2001, pg. 2
* Copy and color bees included with this lesson
* Tape
* Picture of Gordon B. Hinckley for display during the lesson

This lesson can take up to two hours to complete, consider whether or not you would like to split it into two activities or allot more time as a special Saturday or summer activity.

Prayerfully read through the above listed article and mark several points that you would especially like for your children to remember.

Tell the children that this message is directly from the prophet to them as youth. Help them understand that he loves them and is speaking to them. Show each of the bees, and discuss them in order of mention from the article. Have the children occasionally read portions of President Hinckley's words that you marked earlier.

When all the bees have been placed have the children repeat them with you several times and allow them to voice their opinions on which they like best.

Note: For simplicity and clarity, this lesson is taken from President Hinckley's original talk on the 6 B's as presented on November 12, 2000. If your feel prompted to do so, you can expand this lesson to include the other 3 B's later added in his book "Way to Be! 9 Ways to Be Happy and Make Something of Your Life" Simon & Schuster © 2003.

Activity:
Materials Needed:
* Several sheets of craft foam (each piece can make 6 flowers, but you will want a variety of colors available)

* Several copies of the flower patterns on cardstock and cut out for use as patterns
* 9 black pipe cleaners
* 6 yellow pipe cleaners
* 3 white pipe cleaners
* 9 green pipe cleaners
* 12 Hershey Kisses®, 6 to eat 6 for the craft
* 1 copy of the "6 B" word strips
* 1 3 or 4 inch clay flower pot or 1 plastic or foam cup (preferably wide mouth)
* 1 strip of modeling clay
* 1 low-temperature glue gun and glue sticks
* 1 permanent marker
* 1 pair of craft scissors
* 1 pencil
* Several pens for tracing flowers
* Easter grass or other craft item to fill flowerpots
* Various craft supplies for decorating the flowerpot

Materials listed are for one complete pot of flowers, be sure to increase your supplies according to the number of children in your group.

Assist the children in tracing and cutting 6 foam flowers then punching through two holes in the center of each flower—far enough apart that they won't tear through.

Cut one green stem into two even pieces, set aside one piece for the next flower.

Fold one whole green stem in half, poke the ends into the holes in the center of one flower and pull through until the folded end meets the flower petals. Begin twisting the two halves together till about 1/3 of it is twisted. Stop and put aside for a moment.

Take the small green stem and bend the ends into the middle, making two loops and twist the ends around the middle to stabilize them. Place the middle of the two loops into the stem of your flower just below the area that is already twisted, then finish twisting the rest of the stem so that the leaves you made are held into place.

Assemble all six flowers in this manner, and then set them aside.

Take one yellow and one black stem and twist them together from end to end.

Cut one white cleaner into two equal halves and set aside one half. Fold the other half in the same manner as the flower leaves, this time they will create wings.

Begin wrapping the yellow and black stems tightly around a pencil. When approximately half of the stem is wrapped place the wings underneath the next portion to be wrapped (slightly in from either end) then continue wrapping the rest of the stem. Apply a little extra pressure to the end of the stem to hold it in place. Gently slide your bee's body off the end of the pencil and set aside.

Take one black stem and cut it into two equal halves, setting one aside. Fold the remaining piece in half. Curl the free ends over slightly. Slide the folded end into the open center of the bee body to create a stinger and antenna on either end. The antenna ends may be curled separately around a pencil if curled ends are desired. Complete six bees in this manner and set them aside.

Cut off six word strips. Take six Kisses® and gently open their foil wrapper so that the candy and Hershey's® logo strip can be removed. Hold a word strip in one hand so that the words face up and the blank end can be placed down into the empty wrapper. Replace the candy on top of the word strip and gently fold the aluminum back around the candy. Repeat this process for each of the six Kisses®. Gently fold the word strip down slightly so that the words can be read.

Use the glue gun to glue a Kiss® into the center of each flower. Glue a bee beside each candy.

Soften a strip of Modeling Clay and mold it into a thick circle to be pressed into the bottom of your flowerpot. Stick the ends of your flowers down into the clay to secure them into your pot. Fill the rest of the pot with Easter grass to take up the extra space and hold your arrangement into place.

Write the words "The Prophet's Words for Me" on their flowerpots and allow them to decorate the pot if time allows.

Use this lesson to reinforce:

* *My Gospel Standards*
* *Faith in God*, learning and living the gospel
* Cub Scouts Wolf, Bear and Webelos religious requirements
* *Family Home Evening Resource Book*, lesson ideas "gratitude", "honesty", "humility", "learning", and "listening"
* *Primary 1*, lesson 18
* *Primary 3*, lesson 8
* *Primary 4*, lesson 41
* *Primary 5*, lesson 15
* *Primary 6*, lesson 27
* *Aaronic Priesthood 1*, lesson 12
* *Aaronic Priesthood 3*, lesson 24
* *D&C and Church History Gospel Doctrine Manual*, lesson 37

Prayerful
Grateful

Smart
True

Clean
Humble

Be Grateful
Be Smart
Be Clean
Be True
Be Humble
Be Prayerful
Be Grateful
Be Smart
Be Clean
Be True
Be Humble
Be Prayerful
Be Grateful
Be Smart
Be Clean
Be True
Be Humble
Be Prayerful
Be Grateful
Be Smart
Be Clean
Be True
Be Humble
Be Prayerful

Be Grateful
Be Smart
Be Clean
Be True
Be Humble
Be Prayerful
Be Grateful
Be Smart
Be Clean
Be True
Be Humble
Be Prayerful
Be Grateful
Be Smart
Be Clean
Be True
Be Humble
Be Prayerful
Be Grateful
Be Smart
Be Clean
Be True
Be Humble
Be Prayerful

Five
Becoming a Scripture Sleuth

Scripture: "And when ye shall receive these things, I would exhort you that ye would ask God, the Eternal Father, in the name of Christ, if these things are not true; and if ye shall ask with a sincere heart, with real intent, having faith in Christ, he will manifest the truth of it unto you, by the power of the Holy Ghost. And by the power of the Holy Ghost ye may know the truth of all things."

—Moroni 10:4-5

Song: "Search, Ponder and Pray," *Children's Songbook*, pg. 109.

Treat: Miniature chocolate bars

Lesson:
Materials Needed:
* Copies of the "I Can Read the Book of Mormon" assignment page and coloring sheet for each child
* Scripture Sleuth Check-Off Sheet ready for display, this sheet is for marking off the children's answers to the clues. It is used as a method of keeping track of whether or not they are reading and understanding.
* Copy of the Book of Mormon for each child (you might want to insure ahead of time that each child has his or her own personal copy of the Book of Mormon in their home. If they do not, consider obtaining paper back copies for the children to use with this study program).
* 15 index cards: label each with a book name from the Book of Mormon, hide them around the room where you meet
* Photocopy of "Ye" and "Yea" cards on cardstock quality paper, multiply the number of children in your group by three to determine how many copies you will need for the game. Cut apart the cards and mix them up well.

This lesson is meant to be a fun and gentle introduction to the Book of Mormon and how to use the scriptures. Spend some time at the beginning of the meeting introducing the reading program. Show them the check-off sheet and the clues that they will need to find the answers to as they read. Help them to feel excitement, not discouragement at the task you are asking them to complete. Then spend the rest of the evening completing the following "Getting to know you" Book of Mormon activities.

Ask the children if they can find 15 word cards hidden around the room.

When they have been found tell them that it is their job to see if they can put them in order according to their place in the Book of Mormon. Allow them to make guesses and attempts, they may even ask for a Book of Mormon and try to follow the pages through. Then, show them the Table of Contents page at the front of the book and explain its usefulness in locating sections, allow them to put the cards in the correct order using this as a reference. Learning the song "The Books of the Book of Mormon" *Children's Songbook* pg. 119 is also a fun way for them to become familiar with their order.

Write the word "Cleave" on the board then let the children guess what it might mean.

Show the children the Index and locate "Cleave" in it on page 52. Point out that a definition or similar word is given in parentheses and places where that word is used in the scriptures are listed.

Allow the children to choose one of the references to look up while helping them to understand how the references are listed according to book and chapter then allow them to look up their chosen verse.

When they have found the verse, using the Table of Contents if necessary, show them the small letter markings within the verse and explain that they can be used to help them understand a scripture even better.

These are called footnotes and contain more definitions, clarifications, and other places to look for the same types of information that you are studying. Let them choose several footnotes from the page to look at.

Tell the children that as they read they will see a lot of words that they may not know, its ok, but they can use the things they've learned to help them understand it better. Assure them that they can always ask a grown-up for help understanding something. The scriptures are important lessons from Heavenly Father and He really wants to be able to speak to us through them.

Lastly show them that there are two words that they will see a lot, which look almost the same but mean two different things. Print "YE" and "YEA" on the board and ask them what the difference is.

Help them understand the different pronunciations then tell them their meanings. YE is used as a formal "you" and YEA is used as we would use words like "and so" or "then" to carry on a thought we want to emphasize.

Then play a version of "Hands Down" with the cards you created. The children sit in a circle and you deal the cards out one at a time, face up, into a pile in the middle, in a rapid manner. They are to watch and see how quickly they can slap their hands down onto the pile when the word "YEA" appears and do nothing when they see "YE". The child, whose hand is first on the pile, collects those cards and places them in front of him. Whoever has the most cards at the end of the game is the winner.

If time permits you might also want the children to act out the story of Lehi and his family leaving Jerusalem and obtaining the brass plates (1 Nephi 1-4) so that they can remember and understand where the Book of Mormon originally came from.

Activity:

Materials Needed:

* Copy of the Book of Mormon for each child
* Index cards, from above, with the books of the Book of Mormon on them
* Bag of miniature chocolate bars

Hold a Scripture book chase.
Shuffle the index cards and place them face down in front of you.
Draw a card and read it out loud to the children. To keep it interesting you might want to re-shuffle it into the stack after it's been read.
Then let them search through their scriptures until they find that book.
As they raise their hand to announce they have found the book, toss them a chocolate treat.

Use this lesson to reinforce:
* *My Gospel Standards*
* *Faith in God*, general requirements and learning and living the gospel
* Cub Scouts Wolf, Bear and Webelos religious requirements
* *Family Home Evening Resource Book*, lesson 4
* *Book of Mormon Gospel Doctrine Manual*, lesson 1 and 48
* *Primary 4*, lesson 1 and 44
* *Primary 5*, lesson 3 and 10
* *D&C and Church History Gospel Doctrine Manual*, lesson 4
* *Gospel Principles*, chapter 10
* *Aaronic Priesthood 1*, lesson 33
* *Young Women 1*, lesson 27

I Can Read the Book of Mormon
Do you want to be a Scripture Super Sleuth?
The introduction to the Book of Mormon carries this invitation: "We invite all men everywhere to read the Book of Mormon, to ponder in their hearts the message it contains, and then to ask God, the Eternal Father, in the name of Christ if the book is true. Those who pursue this course and ask in faith will gain a testimony of its truth and divinity by the power of the Holy Ghost." (See Moroni 10:3-5)
Everyone can read this special book and feel its wonderful power, even you. The secret? All it takes is a little time and a desire to learn.
If you begin now and read just a few pages each day, you can read the whole Book of Mormon in one year! As you go, we'll give you clues to look for. If you can find the answers, at the end of the year you will be a Super Scripture Sleuth and you'll earn a special certificate for your room!
But more important than that will be the chance you've had to let the Holy Ghost tell you for yourself just how special this book is.
Here is your weekly assignment list. As you read each assignment, color the number in on your record so you can see your progress and don't forget to turn in the answers to your clues!

Scripture Super Sleuth Assignments and Clues

Week 1—Title Page, Introduction, Testimonies of Three and Eight Witnesses, Testimony of Joseph Smith, Explanation
What tools did Joseph Smith need to be able to translate the Book of Mormon?

Week 2—1 Nephi 1-5
Name the servant of Laban who joined Lehi and his family in the wilderness.

Week 3—1 Nephi 6-10
Who would not eat of the fruit of the tree in Lehi's dream?

Week 4—1 Nephi 11-14
When the Spirit shows Nephi his father's vision, where was he taken that he'd never been before?

Week 5—1 Nephi 15-17
What did Nephi break that made his brothers mad at him?

Week 6—1 Nephi 18-22
How many days was Nephi tied up while sailing toward the Promised Land?

Week 7—2 Nephi 1-3
Find the verse that talks about opposition in all things.

Week 8—2 Nephi 4-7
When Nephi and his people resettled to the land of Nephi, they took the Brass plates and the Liahona with them. What other important item did they take?

Week 9—2 Nephi 8-10
How many times is the word "awake" used in these chapters?

Week 10—2 Nephi 11-16
Name three people that Nephi testifies had seen Jesus Christ.

Week 11—2 Nephi 17-24
Which chapter is a prophecy about Jesus' birth?

Week 12—2 Nephi 25-27
Fill in the blanks. "And we talk of _____, we rejoice in _____, we preach of _____, we prophesy of ______ and we write according to our prophecies, that our _____ may know to what source they may look for a remission of their sins."

Week 13—2 Nephi 28-30
Which scripture talks about learning line upon line, precept upon precept?

Week 14—2 Nephi 31-33
What must we feast upon to obtain eternal life?

Week 15—Jacob 1-4
How can we know if something is true?

Week 16—Jacob 5-7
How many visits did the Lord make to his vineyard in the story about the tame and wild olive trees?

Week 17—Enos, Jarom, Omni, Words of Mormon
Where was Enos when he prayed for forgiveness all day and into the evening?

Week 18—Mosiah 1-3
Name the three sons of King Benjamin

Week 19—Mosiah 4-8
Following King Benjamin's message from the tower, his people were given a new name. What was their new name?

Week 20—Mosiah 9-17
How was Abinadi protected from the wicked priests while he delivered his message?

Week 21—Mosiah 18-24
True or False. When we are baptized, we make a promise that we will serve God and keep his commandments.

Week 22—Mosiah 25-29
What happed to Alma that made him sorry for his sins?

Week 23—Alma 1-4
How many people had joined the church by the seventh year of the reign of judges?

Week 24—Alma 5-7
According to Alma, whose image should we have in our countenance?

Week 25—Alma 8-12
Who became Alma's missionary companion?

Week 26—Alma 13-16
What did the wicked people do in front of Alma and Amulek to try and make them stop sharing the gospel?

Week 27—Alma 17-22
Who was the king over the land where Ammon went on his mission?

Week 28—Alma 23-29
Why did they Anti-Nephi-Lehi's bury their swords and weapons of war?

Week 29—Alma 30-33
Alma taught the Zoramites a lesson about faith. What did he compare faith to?

Week 30—Alma 34-35
Fill in the blank. "For behold this life is the time for men to prepare __________."

Week 31—Alma 36-42
Whose testimony is found in Alma 36?

Week 32—Alma 43-51
When Moroni tore his coat in two pieces to make a flag he called "the Title of Liberty", what did he write on it?

Week 33—Alma 52-58
How many of Helaman's stripling sons were killed in battle?

Week 34—Alma 59-63
Who was the Nephite ship builder that sailed to the land northward with many people and was never heard from again?

Week 35—Helaman 1-4
What did the Nephites who went northward build their houses out of?

Week 36—Helaman 5-9
What group of wicked men was organized into a band of robbers and murders that received secret oaths and covenants from the devil?

Week 37—Helaman 10-12
What power did Heavenly Father bless Nephi with because of his faithfulness?

Week 38—Helaman 13-16
Which prophet announced when Christ would be born?

Week 39—3 Nephi 1-5
Who was Lachoneus?

Week 40—3 Nephi 6-10
What is the reward for those who repent and come unto Christ like a little child?

Week 41—3 Nephi 11-14
Where does the story of Christ's appearance to the people of the American Continent begin?

Week 42—3 Nephi 15-18
Which chapter tells the story of Jesus blessing the children?

Week 43—3 Nephi 19-23
Whose words are we supposed to search diligently because Jesus told us they are great?

Week 44—3 Nephi 24-30
How many of the twelve disciples were promised that they could stay on earth to preach the gospel until the Second Coming?

Week 45—4 Nephi 1
What did the Holy Ghost command Ammaron to do with the records he was keeping?

Week 46—Mormon 1-5
How old was Mormon when he became leader of the Nephite armies?

Week 47—Mormon 6-9
How did Mormon survive the final battle at Cumorah?

Week 48—Ether 1-5
How many barges did Jared and his people build?

Week 49—Ether 6-10
How many days were the Jaredite barges on the water on the way to the Promised Land?

Week 50—Ether 11-15
What was the Jaredite name for the Hill Cumorah?

Week 51—Moroni 1-8
Fill in the blank: Charity is ______________

Week 52—Moroni 9-10
Where are we exhorted to ask God about what we have read in the Book of Mormon?

Scripture Super Sleuth Answer Key

1. The Urim and Thummim (The Testimony of Joseph Smith)
2. Zoram (1 Nephi 4:35)
3. Laman and Lemuel (1 Nephi 8:35)
4. An exceedingly high mountain (1 Nephi 11:1)
5. His steel bow (1 Nephi 16:18)
6. Four (1 Nephi 18:14-15)
7. 2 Nephi 2:11
8. The Sword of Laban (2 Nephi 5:14)
9. Seven (2 Nephi 8:9, 17, 24 and 9:47)
10. Isaiah, Nephi and Jacob (2 Nephi 11:2-3)
11. 2 Nephi 19
12. Christ, Christ, Christ, Christ, children (2 Nephi 25:26)
13. 2 Nephi 28:30
14. The Word of Christ (2 Nephi 31:20)
15. Through the Spirit (Jacob 4:13)
16. Four (Jacob 5)
17. The forest (Enos 1:3)
18. Mosiah, Helorum, Helaman (Mosiah 1:2)
19. The Children of Christ (Mosiah 5:7)
20. The power of God (Mosiah 13:2-6)
21. True (Mosiah 18:10)
22. He saw an angel that spoke to him (Mosiah 27:18)
23. 3,500 (Alma 4:5)
24. God's (Alma 5:14, 19)
25. Amulek (Alma 8:30-32)
26. Believers were stoned and burned to death (Alma 14:7-8)
27. Lamoni (Alma 17:20-21)
28. It showed that they never wanted to fight again (Alma 24:17)
29. A seed (Alma 32:28)
30. To meet God (Alma 34:32)
31. Alma the Younger (Alma 36)
32. In memory of our God, our religion, our freedom, our peace, wives and children (Alma 46:12-13)
33. None (Alma 56:56)
34. Hagoth (Alma 63:5-8)
35. Cement (Helaman 3:7)
36. Gadianton Robbers (Helaman 6:18)
37. Sealing Power (Helaman 10:7)
38. Samuel the Lamanite (Helaman 14:1-2)
39. Chief Judge and governor over the land (3 Nephi 1:1) and chief captain over the armies (3 Nephi 3:17)
40. The kingdom of God (3 Nephi 9:22)
41. 3 Nephi 11
42. 3 Nephi 17
43. Isaiah (3 Nephi 23:1)
44. Three (3 Nephi 28:2-7)
45. Hide them (4 Nephi 1:48)
46. Sixteen (Mormon 2:2)
47. He fell down wounded and the Lamanites passed him by (Mormon 6:10)
48. Eight (Ether 3:1)
49. 344 (Ether 6:11)
50. Ramah (Ether 15:11)
51. The pure love of Christ (Moroni 7:47)
52. Moroni 10:4-5

Ye	Ye
Ye	Ye
Yea	Yea
Ye	Ye

Book of Mormon check-off sheet

Check-off each week as it is completed

Name	1	2	3	4	5	6	7	8	9	10	11	12	13	14	15	16	17	18	19	20	21	22	23	24	25	26	27	28	29	30	31	32	33	34	35	36	37	38	39	40	41	42	43	44	45	46	47	48	49	50	51	52

I CAN READ
THE BOOK
OF MORMON

Super Scripture Sleuth Award
Presented to

Six
An Interview with the Deacon's Quorum

Materials Needed:

Give a copy of the following interview sheet to each boy prior to their twelfth birthday and arrange for them to visit a Young Men's activity where they will have a chance to meet and talk to some of the boys. Encourage them to use the back of their interview paper to record their own thoughts and feelings about entering this program.

Use this lesson to reinforce:

* *Faith in God*, preparing for the priesthood
* *Family Home Evening Resource Book*, lesson 30
* *D&C and Church History Gospel Doctrine Manual*, lessons 8 and 25
* *Primary 3*, lesson 6
* *Primary 5*, lessons 8 and 47
* *Aaronic Priesthood 1*, lesson 37
* *Aaronic Priesthood 3*, lesson 49
* *Gospel Principles,* chapter 17

An Interview with the Deacon's Quorum

How many deacons are there?__________

What are their names?

____________ ____________

____________ ____________

____________ ____________

____________ ____________

When are activities held?

____

What are they like?

____

Who are the leaders? ____________

____

____________ ____________

Who are the advisors? ____________

____

____________ ____________

Have you been on a youth temple trip? __________

What was it like?

____

What was it like the first time you passed the sacrament?

____

____

What is your favorite thing about Young Mens?

____

____

Seven

The Story of the Aaronic Priesthood

Scripture: "Upon you my fellow servants, in the name of Messiah, I confer the Priesthood of Aaron, which holds the keys of the ministering of angels, and of the ministering of angels, an of the gospel of repentance, and of baptism by immersion for the remission of sins; and this shall never be taken again from the earth until the sons of Levi do offer again an offering unto the Lord in righteousness."

—Joseph Smith-History 1:69

Song: "The Priesthood Is Restored," *Children's Songbook*, pg. 89.

Treat: Johnny cakes, mush or other foods appropriate to the era of Joseph Smith and the restoration

Lesson:

Materials Needed:

* Chalkboard and Chalk
* Scriptures for each child
* Gospel art picture #407 "John the Baptist confers the Aaronic Priesthood"
* Copies of the *Aaronic Priesthood handbook:* Fulfilling Our Duty to God (Deacon) pg. 7 for each child

Show the gospel art picture and ask the boys if they know what is being depicted. Have them open their scriptures to Joseph Smith-History 1:68-73. Take turns reading the story of the restoration, and then let the children act out the events as they are written.

Then, read over D&C 13, 20:57-60, 107:20 and Fulfilling Our Duty to God with the children. Stop and list items on the chalkboard, as they are read about, that are part of a deacon's duties or responsibility regarding their priesthood

End with your testimony of the blessings of holding the priesthood and the honor of being able to act in the name of Jesus Christ

Activity:

Materials Needed:

* White or Off-white cotton fabric pieces for each child
* Crayons
* Hot iron
* Plain paper
* Aluminum foil

The fabric pieces should be cut by previously determining what form the finished product will take. Cut them to appropriate sizes to be framed, sewn into pillows or pillowcases, or even wall hangings, etc.

Have children draw a picture on their piece of cloth. It should be either a depiction of something from the story of the restoration of the Aaronic Priesthood or a picture of themselves doing something to honor their priesthood. They should color rather heavily to get a lot of color into the cloth.

After the picture is complete, place a clean piece of paper underneath the fabric and cover the picture with a piece of aluminum foil. Press a hot iron over the picture for at least 30 seconds to seal the picture into the fabric permanently.

Use this lesson to reinforce:
* *Faith in God*, developing talents and preparing for the priesthood
* *Family Home Evening Resource Book*, lesson 30
* *D&C and Church History Gospel Doctrine Manual*, lessons 8 and 25
* *Primary 3*, lesson 6
* *Primary 5*, lessons 8 and 47
* *Aaronic Priesthood 1*, lesson 37
* *Aaronic Priesthood 3*, lesson 49
* *Young Women 3*, lessons 12 and 14
* *Gospel Principles*, chapter 17

Eight
Jesus Loves the Little Children

Scripture: "And when he had said these words, he wept, and the multitude bare record of it, and he took their little children, one by one, and blessed them, and prayed unto the Father for them. And when he had done this he wept again; And he spake unto the multitude, and said unto them: Behold your little ones. And as they looked to behold they cast their eyes towards heaven, and they saw the heavens open, and they saw angels descending out of heaven as it were in the midst of fire; and they came down and encircled those little ones about, and they were encircled about with fire; and the angels did minister unto them."

—3 Nephi 17:21-24

Song: "Jesus Love the Little Children," *Children's Songbook*, pg. 59.

Treat: Peanut butter play-dough.

Lesson:

Materials Needed:

* Double pocket portfolios with paper fasteners for each child
* Notebook paper, several sheets for each child
* Several copies of the family information sheet for each child, hold punched to fit in the portfolios
* Multiple books on activities for young children from your local library
* Writing utensils for each child
* Markers

If available in your area, have someone come in to do a brief course in first aid including choking and rescue breathing for young children. Or, try to obtain pamphlets from your local Red Cross or hospital for the children to place in their folders.

Show the children the folders and papers. Tell them that they are going to assemble a "babysitting notebook" where they can keep track of important information about the families with young children that they help or play with. The notebook will also keep ideas of things to do with them. Remind them that they need to get the parents permission to do the things they plan and try to bring their own supplies when possible.

Help them spend time putting together the notebook and decorating the cover. Then spend time copying ideas from the books that you brought onto their paper. As they work talk to them about caring for young children and how to show love for them.

You might want to arrange a time for your children to help out with a Relief Society children's class or other event where they can try some of the activities they liked and have written down.

Also spend some time singing the activity songs from the Children's Songbook and other rhymes and games.

Recommended books:
* *Things to do with Toddlers and Twos* by Karen Miller
* *The Rainy Day Activity Book* by Jennifer Rader
* *Wonderplay: Interactive & Developmental Games, Crafts & Creative Activities for Infants, Toddlers & Preschoolers* by Fretta Reitzes, et al
* *Preschool Play and Learn: 150 Fun Games and Learning Activities for Preschoolers from Three to Six Years* by Penny Warner.

Activity:

Materials Needed:
* Peanut butter
* Honey
* Powdered milk
* Coconut, granola, mini-chips, sprinkles etc.
* Paper lunch bags
* Craft supplies
* Glue
* Scissors
* Markers or crayons

Help the children construct paper bag puppets to keep with their babysitting supplies. Then, mix up some edible play-dough and play.

Mix 2/3-cup peanut butter with 1/2 cup honey and 1cup powdered milk. Children can play; decorate with coconut, granola and mini chips then eat.

Use this lesson to reinforce:
* *Faith in God*, serving others
* Cub Scouts Bear Achievement 11
* *Young Women 1*, lesson 40 and 45
* *Primary 1*, lessons 24, 33 and 36
* *Primary 2*, lesson 32
* *Family Home Evening Resource Book*, lessons 17 and 23

Family Profile Sheet

Family Name:

Children's Name and ages:

Parent's Emergency Contact Phone Numbers:

Phone Number of Close Neighbor for Emergencies:

Emergencies Call: 911
Poison Control Phone Number:

Any Allergies of Children:

Special Family Rules:

Nine
Writing a Letter

Scripture: "This is a true saying, If a man desire the office of a bishop, he desireth a good work . . ."

—Timothy 3:1

Song: "Our Bishop," *Children's Songbook*, pg. 135.

Treat: Bishop's Bread—this was a traditional treat made by English families to serve only to the Bishop when he visited their homes. Recipes can be found on the Internet.

Lesson:
Materials Needed:
* Chalkboard and Chalk or other writing display
* Notebook paper
* Pencils and pens
* Tape
* Stationary and envelope

On the left side of the board, write a short sample letter. Include the date, greeting, body of the letter and a proper closing. Leave an open space in the middle. On the right draw empty lines for placement of the parts of a letter.

Show the children the letter you wrote and explain the parts to the children.

Tell them that they are going to write a letter to the Bishop of your ward or branch. This letter should be friendly and thank him for the things the children respect about him.

Ask the children to share if they have ever had an interview with the Bishop and what it was like. Share some things you have learned from him as well. Help the children begin to think what his roll as Bishop is and how he can help and serve them. Then, ask the children to write one thing that they like about him on a piece of paper.

Let the children then read what they have written and tape it to the middle of the board. When all the children have read their statements, begin constructing the letter. Ask them to tell you what parts are needed first. Write in the date and help them choose a proper greeting. Then read all their statements out loud again and ask the children to help you decide on an order to write them in the letter. Number them according to their choices then write them on the board. Review the letter with them, add or change anything to help the letter flow right then choose a closing.

Activity:

Materials Needed:

* Craft supplies of your choice
* Cardstock paper
* Envelopes
* Glue
* Scissors
* Crayons or markers
* Pens

Show the children how to fold the paper into a card. Help them write other letters and decorate them. Show them how to properly address the envelopes.

While they are writing their letters, transfer the letter to the bishop onto the stationary you brought and have all the children sign their names.

Use this lesson to reinforce:

* *Faith in God*, serving others
* Cub Scouts Bear Achievements 18 b, and 24 d
* *Family Home Evening Resource Book*, lesson 22 and lesson ideas "gratitude"
* *Primary 2*, lesson 24
* *Primary 7*, lesson 21
* *Aaronic Priesthood 2*, lesson 36
* *Young Women 2*, lesson 11

Ten
Let's Build a Role Model

Scripture: "For I have given you an example, that ye should do as I have done to you."
—St. John 13:15

Song: "Do as I'm Doing," *Children's Songbook*, pg. 276.

Treat: Tootsie Rolls®, for an added touch apply a sticker that reads "I have found a 'Roll' model"

Lesson:
Materials Needed:
* Copy a role model picture and color it for an example.
* Television and video player
* *Family Home Evening Video Supplement* segment "True Friendship"

Prayerfully review the sample labels provided in this manual and then label your picture with attributes that your children most need to recognize in others and develop within themselves. It's helpful if you draw your examples from people the children would know and admire such as the Bishop, a primary teacher or older child, even from the children themselves.

* Head—big from studying hard to learn and grow
* Eyes—always try to see the good in others
* Hair—neat and clean
* Mouth—tries to always be honest and tell the truth, or always has a smile for everyone they see
* Shoulders—wide for helping someone in need
* Hands—callused from working hard in all they do, or they can do a certain talent-i.e. music or craft
* Body—healthy from living the council of the Word of Wisdom
* Legs—extra-long for going the extra mile and doing more than is required of them
* Knees—padded for frequent prayers, showing dependence on the Lord
* Feet—always keep going, even when it's hard

Discuss these attributes with the children; help them understand what makes these character traits valuable and how a person can develop them.

Show the video segment and ask the children to consider the attributes of their closest friends. Did they recognize those things you discussed as being of value in others, can their friends be true role models and want the best for them?

Activity:

Materials Needed:

* Copies of role model picture for each child
* Crayons, colored pencils or markers
* Pencils and pens for each child

Let each child color their picture and help them apply labels of attributes they admire in others.

Help them brain storm ideas on ways they can be more like their role models. They should write their ideas on their pictures as well so that they can have a ready reminder of whom and what they want to be like.

Use this lesson to reinforce:

* *Gospel Standards*
* *Faith in God*, serving others
* *Family Home Evening Resource Book*, lesson 8 and 12 lesson idea "friendship"
* *Primary 1*, lesson 36
* *Primary 2*, lesson 29
* *Young Women 1*, lesson 21

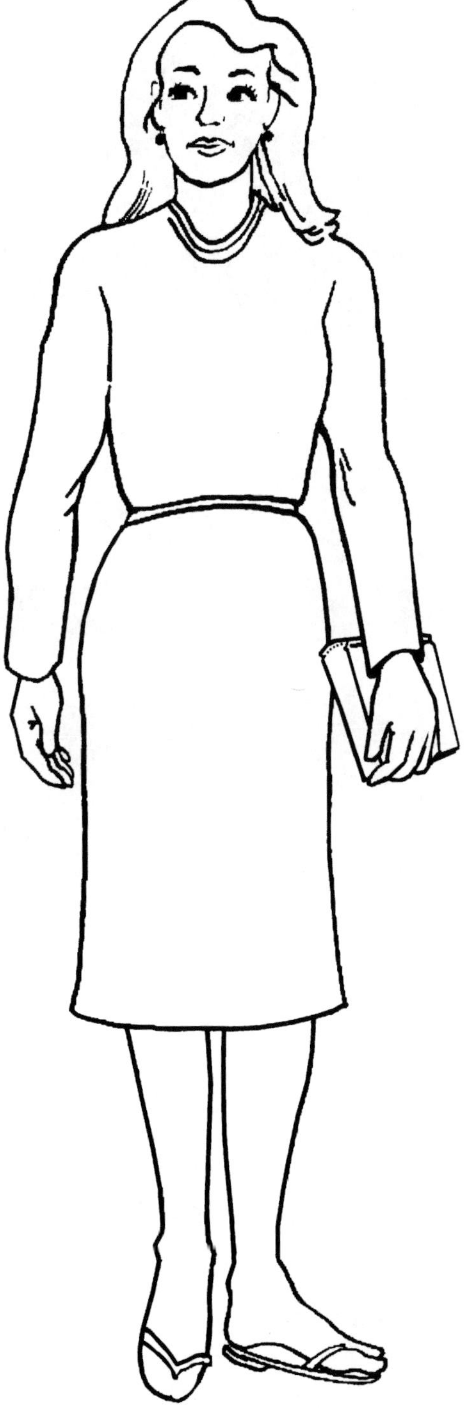

Eleven
Physical Fitness

Scripture: "And all saints who remember to keep and do these sayings, walking in obedience to the commandments, shall receive health in their navel and marrow to their bones; And shall run and not be weary, and shall walk and not faint."

—D&C 89:18, 20

Song: "The Word of Wisdom," *Children's Songbook*, pg. 154.

Treat: Olympic torches—bake cupcakes inside of flat-bottomed ice cream cones. Top with meringue that has been slightly tinted with yellow or orange food coloring and peaked to look like flames. Return to the oven till the peaks have browned slightly.

Lesson:
Materials Needed:
* Chalk and chalkboard
* Large piece of paper
* Paper and writing utensils for each child
* Slips of paper with the individual activities and country of origin listed
* Container for holding papers until they are drawn
* World map

Instruct the children that together you are going to draw a person, divide the body into enough pieces that each child can participate.

Give the paper to the first child and have him draw a head and neck toward the top of the paper. Then fold the paper over so that the drawn portion is not visible but the next person can draw the shoulder area directly below it. Continue folding over the drawn portion and handing the paper to the next child to add the next portion of the body. When the body is complete, unfold the entire paper to show the children what they have drawn.

Share with the children that even though what you have drawn is a little silly, it is unique. Heavenly Father has given each of us a body as part of the plan for our happiness. Each one of us is different and special with unique talents and interests. Each of us has a responsibility to our Heavenly Father to try and develop our minds and bodies in a pleasing manner. Part of that responsibility is learning to take care of our physical bodies.

There are simple rules that we can follow. Have the children think of what kinds of things we need to do to keep our bodies clean and healthy. List them on the chalkboard. If you are working with Wolf Scouts review the seven rules for health listed in their requirements.

Have the children test their endurance at a variety of physical skills such as sit-ups, push-ups, jumping jacks, splits. Wolf Scouts can also pass off skills required for Feats of Skill. Keep a record of their accomplishments on the chalkboard.

Now have them draw a complete picture of themselves and list those things that they can do to keep their bodies clean and healthy.

Share that one of the best ways to keep our bodies healthy is to make sure we get enough exercise. Have them list their favorite games and sports.

Explain that children all over the world have favorite games and sports that they like to play. Show them your container of games. Have each child draw a game from your container. Help them find the country of origin for their game on the map.

Explain that they will have one month in which to find out as much as they can about that game, prepare any needed equipment and practice playing it effectively. At two weeks, you will review with each of them and provide any needed help. In one month, or a similarly scheduled time, they will be in charge of teaching their game to the other primary children at a quarterly primary activity day of international games.

If it is not feasible in your area to hold a quarterly activity of this nature, use several activity nights and have the children just teach each other. Approximately 30 minutes is required for instruction and play of each game.

A variety of games are listed here. Please keep in mind any special needs children you may have in your group and help them find a game or activity that they can also feel successful at.

* "Chicken Fight" (Brazil) like flag football, without the ball, and with the use of only one arm.
* "Peteca" (Brazil) similar to shuttlecock but with the use of hand rather than foot.
* "Shuttlecock" (China, Japan, Korea) keeping shuttlecock aloft with only your feet.
* "European Handball" (Denmark) requires a small soccer ball, teams and ball handling above the knees. Many rules apply.
* "Chasqui Relay" (Ecuador, Chile) classic "telephone" set in a relay race.
* "Quilles" (France) bowling with a pendulum.
* "Hoops" (Greece) the player must master keeping the hoop rolling on its side with only one hand or a stick.
* "El Reloj" (Guatemala) jump rope game for 13 players the object is to make a clock and its moving hand.
* "Northland Soccer Ball" (Iceland, Greenland) use a well-worn football to score points by manipulating the ball into a circle.
* "Kulit K'rang" (Indonesia) requires hand-eye coordination and quick reflexes to balance and catch small objects.
* "Hurling" (Ireland) fast and competitive catch and throw game.
* "Palm Ball" (Italy) bouncing a tennis ball between two players.
* "Dakiu" (Japan) ball and paddle team game.
* "Chapete" (Mexico) the original hacky sack game.
* "Indian Kickball" (Mexico) team ball handling through an obstacle course.
* "Comanche Ball and Darts on El Camino Ancho" (Native American Indian) catch and throw of a soft dart with a stick. Played on a steep incline.

* "Wee-ichida" (Native American Indian) ball control with short kicks along a straight or circular path.
* "Rounders" (New Zealand) similar to baseball.
* "Walking Tall" (New Zealand) follow the leader and games of chase on stilts.
* "Apachetas" (Inca, South America) a burden depositing relay race with spatulas and multiple small objects.
* "Apurimac Bridge Obstacle Race" (South America) classic obstacle course.
* "Trier" (Trinidad) requires hand-eye coordination and quick reflexes to balance and catch small objects.

Activity:

Materials Needed:

* Pen and Paper for taking notes
* Large playing area
* World map

Spend some time helping the children identify their country of origin for their games and begin taking down their ideas and thoughts for planning the international game day.

Wet their whistle for game playing with one of the following activities or another of your own choosing.

* "1,2,3, Dragon" (China) Players form a line with hands on the shoulders of the person in front of them. When the person who is the tail of the dragon shouts "1,2,3 Dragon!" the person at the head of the dragon begins to run, twisting and turning about while trying to catch its own tail. If the body breaks, the head moves to the end of the line and play begins again. Each player scores points when it is their turn as the head. Points are scored for every time they were able to catch the tail before the body broke. The player with the most points wins.
* "Pusa At Aso" (Philippines) means "cat and dog". Choose two players to be the cat and dog. The other children form a circle and hold hands. The dog must begin play outside the circle, the cat must be inside. At the signal the dog must begin chasing the cat in, out and around the circle attempting to catch it. The children in the circle try to aid the cat by preventing the dog passage by lowering and raising their arms. They can also challenge the cat's passage as well. When the cat is tagged, the dog and cat return to the circle and choose their successors.

Use this lesson to reinforce:

* *Faith in God*, learning and living the gospel, serving others, developing talents
* Cub Scouts Bear Achievements 15 b and c, Wolf Achievements 1 and 3a
* *Family Home Evening Resource Book*, physical fitness award program, and our cultural heritage
* *Primary 2*, lesson 3
* *Aaronic Priesthood 3*, lesson 27
* *Young Women 1*, lesson 37
* *Young Women 2*, lesson 38

Twelve
A Testimony on My Hand

Scripture: "Remember this, which I tell you before, that you may lay it to heart, and receive that which is to follow. Behold, verily I say unto you, for this cause I have sent you—that you might be obedient, and that your hearts might be prepared to bear testimony of the things which are to come;"

—D&C 58:5-6

Song: "The Church of Jesus Christ," *Children's Songbook*, pg. 77.

Treat: Finger Sandwiches

Lesson:
Materials Needed:
* Chalk
* Eraser
* Chalkboard

Based on the remarks of Sydney S. Reynolds at the special satellite broadcast for children, February 8, 2003.

Begin by asking the children to help you list all the reasons why someone would attend our church.

List the things they think of on the chalkboard.

Help them understand that some of the reasons may be better than others, but sooner or later each of us has to answer the question "Is it true?" for ourselves. Then, that answer becomes our reason for attending and trying to live the commandments.

Explain to the children that the answers we receive to this question are how we gain a testimony.

Everyone, who wants to gain a testimony, has to go through certain steps. But as the Holy Ghost begins to whisper that something is true it makes us happy and we can learn and grow even more.

It's like growing a beautiful flower.

Draw a slightly bumpy horizontal line on the chalkboard to represent soil. Tell the children that the most basic thing they need to know is who God is. Ask the children to list some of the things they have learned about God. Help them to recognize the peaceful feeling they have as you discuss that God is our Heavenly Father, that we once lived with Him, and we wanted to be like Him. This is like finding good, fertile soil to grow our seeds in. Assist them in pointing out ways that we can see and feel each day that Heavenly Father loves us and wants us to be happy.

Add a teardrop seed under the ground you drew. Tell the children that this seed is like each of us as we come to know Heavenly Father. We feel warm and safe and we can feel his love for us, just like a seed that has found good, rich soil to grow in.

After we have a testimony of Heavenly Father and His love for each of us, we remember how much we wanted to be like Him. He sent us here to earth, or planted us in such good soil, so we could grow and learn and become more like He is.

Draw multiple thin roots coming out from the bottom of the seed. Tell the children that because Heavenly Father loves us and knew there would be times we would make mistakes, He sent someone special to help us. He is our example and cleanses us from the things we do wrong and the hurts we feel. Allow the children to voice who this special person is. Jesus Christ is our special friend and brother, sent by Heavenly Father to show us how to return to Him. As each of our seeds begins to recognize how special Jesus is to us, and how much He loves us, we begin to grow. We send out many strong roots that will feed and support our plant as it grows. Without strong roots, our flowers could not grow properly or be able to stand when it rained or the winds were strong.

Jesus Christ is called our firm foundation. When we love Him and understand what He can do for us, this knowledge gives us the strength we need to stand strong when other things would have us wither or blow away. Once again, help the children recognize the feelings the Holy Ghost sends when you reverently talk about Jesus Christ.

Draw a stem out of the top of the seed, emerging above the ground. Because Jesus Christ lived very long ago and His teachings got lost along the way, we needed someone who could help us know exactly what Jesus wanted us to know about His church. Ask the children to tell you the story of a boy who knelt in a grove of trees to find out which church he should join. Help the children complete this story, including the coming forth of the Book of Mormon (See Joseph Smith-History). Remind them that because of these events, we know exactly what Jesus wants us to be like.

Add a few leaves off the sides of the stem. Because Joseph Smith restored the truth and translated the Book of Mormon we can be members of Christ's true church today. It's just like the Church that Jesus established when He came to earth. This Church is the same no matter where you go because they all come from the same root and stem.

Draw the center of a daisy on top of the stem. Assure the children that even though Jesus Christ is not here with us today, He would never leave us without someone to look to for answers. A prophet, called by God, speaks for Him and helps us to always know how we can be more like Heavenly Father.

Ask the children to list some of the things the prophets have told us we need to do. With each suggestion add a petal to your flower.

Every time the prophet speaks we have an opportunity to find out if what he has told us is true or not. As we learn each new thing, it becomes part of our testimony. With each part, our flower becomes more beautiful and precious to us.

Remind them one more time, with your testimony, of the special feelings they have felt during this discussion.

A thing this beautiful can and should be shared with others. If we share it, it helps our own feelings grow, and also helps other people's flowers grow.

How do you know when you should share your testimony with someone and how do you know what to say?

Allow the children to share their thoughts and ideas, then reinforce that the most important reason for sharing a testimony is because you feel those warm feelings from the Spirit and want to share it with others.

When we give a testimony we don't need to tell stories or talk for a long time, simple feelings and thoughts often help the Holy Ghost touch others better than lots of words or just talking because you like to, or someone dared you to. We can practice sharing our testimonies in our primary classes and with our families or when we're asked to give talks in primary. Once we learn how, and know what the Spirit feels like, it will be easier. But most importantly we know even more that this church really is true.

Encourage the children to practice their testimonies at appropriate times, and to record their thoughts in their journals as their testimonies grow

For more discussion on helping children know when to bare testimony refer to: Carl B. Cook, "When Children Want to Bear Testimony," *Ensign*, Dec. 2002, 29

Activity:

Materials Needed:

* Crayons, colored pencils or markers
* Copies of the finger puppets, for each child, on card stock quality paper
* Glue
* Scissors

Allow Children to color their finger puppets, and then cut them out.

Glue the strips on the back as shown in the diagram and allow them to dry while you introduce the following rhyme. Each of the sentences in the middle stanza represents a finger on the hand, beginning with the thumb.

A Testimony on My Hand

I count my fingers, one through five,
And count the truths I know.
I say them in a little rhyme,
And this is how it goes.

I have a Heavenly Father,
Whose love is sure and true.
He sent His Son to help me,
And show me what to do.
When Joseph knelt in prayer,
The truth could be restored.
Christ's Church is on the earth today.
And our prophet's called by the Lord.

These five things on my hand,
Help me learn and know.
They bring joy to my heart,
And help my testimony grow.

Use this lesson to reinforce:
* *My Gospel Standards*
* *Faith in God*, testimony
* Cub Scouts Wolf, Bear and Webelos religious requirements
* *Family Home Evening Resource Book*, lesson 16
* *Aaronic Priesthood 1*, lesson 36
* *Aaronic Priesthood 3*, lesson 45
* *Young Women 1*, lesson 26
* *Young Women 2*, lesson 27
* *Young Women Personal Progress,* testimony
* *Primary 4*, lesson 22 and 44
* *Primary 5*, lesson 46
* *Primary 6*, lesson 41
* *Primary 7*, lesson 37

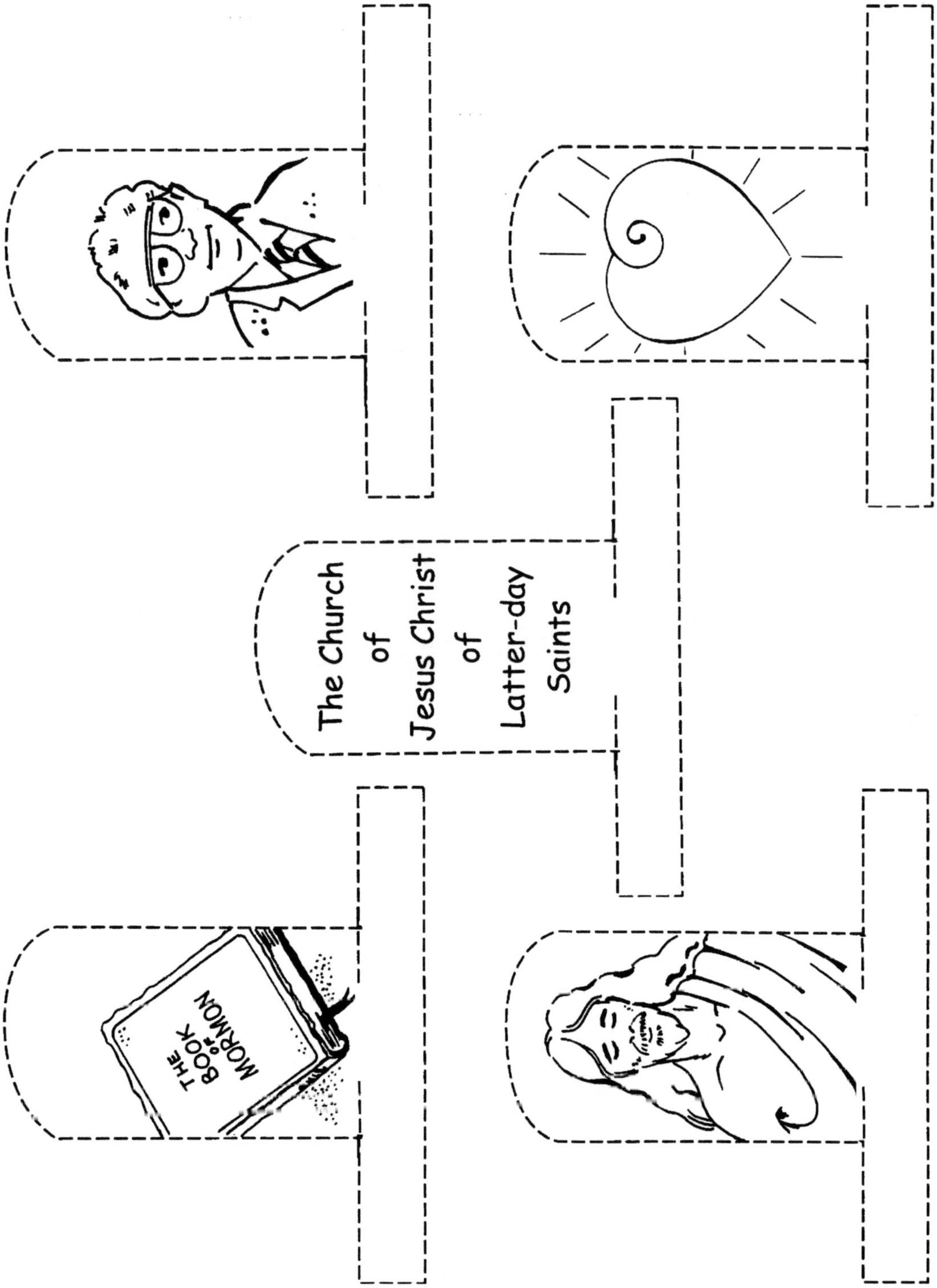
The Church
of
Jesus Christ
of
Latter-day
Saints
THE
BOOK
OF
MORMON

Thirteen
Ready for Church

Scripture: "And that thou mayest more fully keep thyself unspotted from the world, thou shalt go to the house of prayer and offer up thy sacraments upon my holy day;"

—D&C 59:9-10

Song: "When I Go to Church," *Children's Songbook*, pg. 157.

Treat: Sundaes

Lesson:

Materials Needed:

* Chalkboard and chalk or dry erase board and marker
* Pencil and Paper for each child

Write the word "Church" down the left side of your board. Ask the children if they think it is important to go to church. Allow them to voice their opinions and freely express their feelings. Share with them your own feelings and testimony about being able to attend church each week. Express to them that you want them to feel excited about church and get the most out it.

Fill in the statement "Connect with other saints" behind the letter C. Explain that coming to church is our chance to be around people who believe and feel the same way we do about Heavenly Father and Jesus. We make friends and support each other so it's easier to choose the right and not feel alone in our choices.

Write "Honor Heavenly Father" behind the H. Heavenly Father and Jesus Christ have done wonderful things for us. Ask the children to name as many things as they can think of that they are thankful for. Remind them that taking time out to come to church is one way that we can show Heavenly Father and Jesus that they are important to us and we are thankful for all our blessings.

Next write "Understand the Gospel". We attend classes and listen to talks about all kinds of gospel subjects so that we can understand what Heavenly Father wants our lives to be like.

The most important thing we can do at church is to "Renew our Covenants". This means that we come to take the sacrament and remember the promises we have made to Heavenly Father. We think of Jesus Christ as we take the sacrament and feel grateful for the atonement so we can find ways to correct mistakes we have made.

If we do these things when we take the sacrament and listen to our lessons then the spirit can help us hear things that we need to do to be better. Write "Challenges us to do better". We try to learn how we can be more like Jesus as we go to church.

Lastly, write "Have peace". Remind the children of the words to the opening song. Church is a place of happy feelings. The world is full of all kinds of feelings, some happy, some sad, some frustrating, some mad. When we come to church we find happiness that makes all the other feelings and other things that happen to us each week seem better. We still worry and we still do everything else that comes with being able to live on earth, but we get to be reminded that Heavenly Father really does love us, He is there for us, and will help us whenever we need Him.

Ask the children to share stories with you of what it's like to get ready for church in their house and help you make a list of everything that you usually need to do to be ready.

Encourage them to also think of times when things haven't gone right. Has there been a time in his or her family where everything seemed to go wrong, so everyone came to church grumpy? Has anyone had to go to church with out socks on because they couldn't find any? Did someone's brother have to borrow his dad's tie so he could pass the sacrament?

Write the "To Do" list on the chalkboard while reminding them to think of ways the preparations could have gone better or be done ahead of time.

Remind the children of the song "Saturday" *Children's Songbook* pg.196. Sing the words through with the children and notice that the things they thought they had to do are somewhat different from those mentioned in the song, but the message is still the same. There are lots of things we can do on Saturday to make Sunday more special. Try changing the words of the song around to match your children's list. (The object is more fun and lesson reinforcement than perfection!)

Hand each child a paper and pencil. Have them write a goal for the next Sunday on it. This goal should be something that will make getting ready for church easier, or something they want to improve on at church. Then have the children draw a picture of themselves accomplishing their goal. Challenge the children to place their goal somewhere that it will be seen and to try very hard to reach it for one month.

Activity:

Materials Needed (Items listed are for construction of 1 raceway):

* Worn out adult dress clothes, gender appropriate. Include details such as ties, socks or stockings and shoes.
* 1 large cardboard box that a child could stand in and hold at hip level. Cut off the flaps and cover the edges with industrial tape for easier gripping and protection from cuts. For those who are more creative, cover the box in craft paper and decorate it to look like a car.
* 2 chairs or large stationary objects to act as a doorway
* 1 chair to represent a church pew

Each child should dress completely for church, race to the car, get in and "drive" to the chapel, park their car, go through the doors and sit down in the pew. Then they must complete the process in reverse to end their turn.

For less competitive play, use a stopwatch or watch with a second hand to time each child as they complete the course.

For more competitive play, increase the number of raceways and divide children into teams for a more traditional obstacle/relay race.

To preserve the attitude of reverence in your church buildings, this game is best played outside or in the cultural hall where available.

Use this lesson to reinforce:

* *My Gospel Standards*
* *Faith in God*, general requirements
* Cub Scouts Wolf, Bear and Webelos religious requirements, also Wolf Elective 17f
* *Family Home Evening Resource Book*, lesson ideas "reverence"
* *Primary 3*, lesson 40
* *D&C and Church History Gospel Doctrine Manual*, lesson 16
* *Aaronic Priesthood 3*, lesson 29
* *Gospel Principles,* chapter 24

Fourteen
The Ten Commandments

Scripture: "And behold, all that he requires of you is to keep his commandments; and he has promised you that if ye would keep his commandments ye should prosper in the land; and he never doth vary from that which he hath said; therefore, if ye do keep his commandments he doth bless you and prosper you."

—Mosiah 2:22

Song: "The Commandments," *Children's Songbook*, pg. 112 or "Keep the Commandments," *Children's Songbook*, pg. 146.

Treat: Mini muffins

Lesson:

Materials Needed:

* Copy of commandment pages, colored, cut and laminated for durability
* Bibles for each child
* Tape

Help the children locate the Ten Commandments as written in Exodus 20:1-17. As you read through these verses with the children identify each commandment, as it is read, and display the scroll listing that commandment.

Then, one at a time, place the corresponding picture next to the commandment and let the children voice their ideas about what each could mean. Help them clarify and understand the meanings by sharing the scenarios for them to problem solve with, and discuss how the commandments affect their lives each day.

After all the commandments have been reviewed, use the scrolls as a memory game. Match the commandment with its picture and briefly review its meaning once again. As the matches are made, re-hang them in order for use during the activity.

Activity:

Materials Needed:

* Twenty pieces of paper, ten blank, ten numbered individually 1-10
* *Children's Songbook*/tape/CD or other appropriate music
* Music player
* Mini-muffins, enough for at least 4 per child
* Slips of paper numbered 1-10, placed in a grab bag or container
* Tape

Secure the papers to the floor to create a large circle. This will create a cakewalk path. Alternate the numbered and plain papers.

Play music as the children walk around the circle. Stop the music at varying intervals and have the children halt when they don't hear the music. Draw a number out of your grab bag, if a child is standing on that number they must try to name the commandment that corresponds to their number (for a greater challenge remove your display!). If they are able to answer correctly they receive a mini-muffin and must sit out one round while they eat it. Play continues until all the muffins are gone or until everyone has been able to earn at least two muffins. The rest would be fairly divided after play.

Use this lesson to reinforce:
* *My Gospel Standards*
* *Faith in God*, general requirements
* Cub Scouts Wolf, Bear and Webelos religious requirements
* *Family Home Evening Resource Book*, lesson 2
* *Primary 6*, lesson 21

Commandment Scenarios

Commandment #1: When Matthew's older brother came home from college, he said he didn't believe the church was true any more. He thought that it was much more important to be able to learn and study and think for himself. He said he was tired of something he couldn't see or prove existed telling him what he could or couldn't do. He said knowledge was the only God he believed in.

Commandment #2: Sarah just adores a certain movie star. She has his poster all over her room and spends all her money on his movies. She reads all the gossip and books about him. Sometimes she doesn't remember to do things she should like pay her tithing, or pray and read her scriptures. Sometimes she gets in trouble at school for daydreaming about him. On Sunday, the primary had a lesson about the Israelites worshiping a golden calf. Their teacher warned them not to put other things before God, or to pretend that something is a God that isn't, but that's not the same thing as liking a movie star is it?

Commandment #3: One of Jamie's favorite songs on the radio uses one of Heavenly Father's names in it several times, but it's not really a reverent song. She wonders if it's still OK as long as she just ignores those parts and doesn't sing those words when she listens.

Commandment #4: Samantha's cousin is visiting for the weekend. She asks if Samantha will take her to the shopping mall on Sunday.

Commandment #5: James hates it when his mother tells him to clean his room. It seems all she ever does is nag at him. What difference does it make if his room is messy? It's his room right?

Commandment #6: Henry and Josh want to see if they can hit a squirrel with their paintball guns, just to practice. Seth is worried that they might hurt the squirrel. He's also worried that his friends will think he's silly for caring.

Commandment #7: Terry has an older sister who brags about how many boys she's kissed. She says she doesn't want to ever get married and be stuck with just one person forever.

Commandment #8: Last week Justin saw a kid steal a pack of baseball cards from the corner store. He never got caught and he got some really cool cards. Now, Justin thinks it would be ok to take a candy bar since he forgot his lunch.

Commandment #9: Emily told Julia a secret about their friend Robin. Julia wasn't sure if the secret was true or not, but she was pretty sure Robin wouldn't want everyone to know about it. But then she heard someone else talking about Robin and her secret. Would it be all right if she talked to them about it since they seemed to already know?

Commandment #10: Colby's best friend just got a new bike. It's the same bike that Colby had asked for on his last birthday. He hadn't gotten it because his dad said it was too expensive. Colby doesn't think his friend deserves to have such a nice bike when he couldn't have one himself. Colby decided he just wouldn't be his friend anymore.

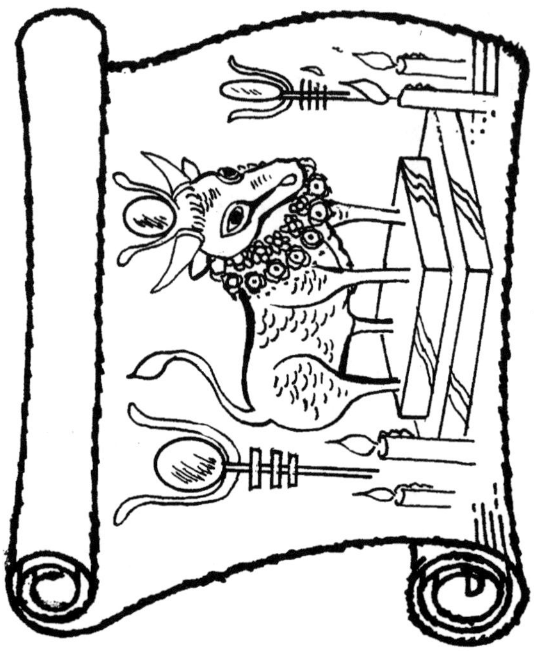

Thou shalt have
no other
gods before me.

Thou shalt not
make unto thee
any graven image.

Thou shalt not take the name of the Lord thy God in vain.

Remember the sabbath day, to keep it holy.

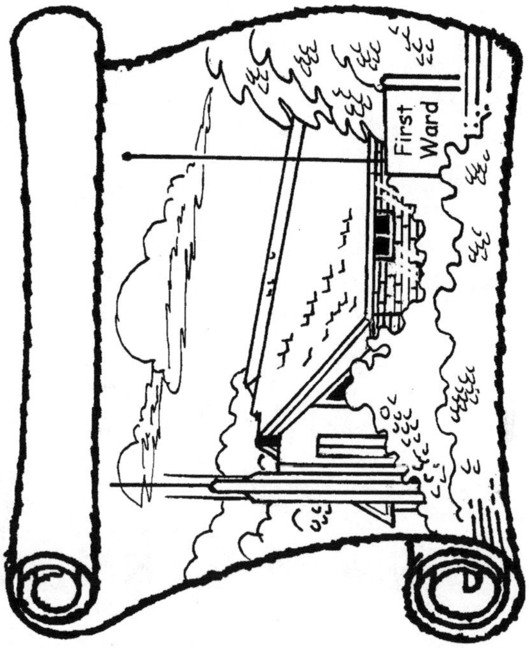

Honour
thy father and
thy mother.

Thou
shalt not
kill.

Thou shalt not
commit
adultery.

Thou
shalt not
steal.

Thou shalt not
bear false
witness.

Thou
shalt not
covet.

Fifteen
An Interview with the Young Women

Materials Needed:

Give a copy of the following interview sheet to each girl prior to their twelfth birthday and arrange for them to visit a Young Women's activity where they will have a chance to meet and talk to some of the girls. Encourage them to use the back of their interview paper to record their own thoughts and feelings about entering this program.

Use this lesson to reinforce:

* *Faith in God*, preparing for Young Women
* *Young Women Personal Progress*, overview of Young Women
* *Young Women 3*, lesson 47

An Interview with the Young Women

How many beehives are there? ____________

What are their names?

____________ ____________

____________ ____________

____________ ____________

____________ ____________

When are activities held?

____

What are they like?

____

Who are the leaders? ______________

____

________________ ________________

Who are the advisors? ______________

____

________________ ________________

Have you been on a youth temple trip? __________

What was it like?

____

Have you been to girl's camp? ____________

What was it like?

____

What is your favorite thing about Young Womens?

____

____

Sixteen
Beautiful Me

Scripture: "But the Lord said unto Samuel, Look not on his countenance, or on the height of his stature; because I have refused him: for the LORD seeth not as man seeth; for man looketh on the outward appearance, but the Lord looketh on the heart."

—1 Samuel 16:7

Song: "My Heavenly Father Loves Me," *Children's Songbook*, pg. 228.

Treat: Small bags of jellybeans with a "beauty pills" label. Call out the colors of the jellybeans but let each girl fill in the traits she wants most to work on as a reminder of her goals.

Lesson:

Materials Needed:

* Gospel art picture #239 "The Resurrected Jesus Christ" or 240 "Jesus The Christ"
* Several sheets of transparency film. Take the picture of Christ and your transparency film to a local copy shop and have them make a light copy of Christ onto the transparency. You want to be able to see another image behind it.
* Mirror large enough to hold your transparent image of Christ, transparency may be cut to fit shape the shape of the mirror.
* Television and video player
* *The Worth of Souls* videocassette set to "Johnny Lingo" (25 minutes)
* A copy of Gordon B. Hinckley's talk "A Prophet's Counsel and Prayer for Youth" Ensign, Jan. 2001, 2.
* A copy of a current "teen" magazine off the news stand
* A copy of The New Era
* Pencil and paper for each child

Give each girl a piece of paper and pencil. Have them fold the paper in half.

Show the girls the mirror you brought with you. Allow each child a chance to view her own reflection. Ask them to think of the things they like best about their appearance. Tell them to write these things down on one half of their paper. As they are writing, suggest something to each girl that is appealing about their outward appearance, pretty eyes, nice hair, pretty smile etc.

Next place your transparency over the mirror and again show it to the girls. Ask them what is different about their image now. Express to them that there is a special beauty that can only come from inside of us. When we are trying to be more like Jesus, it shows in who we are and how others see us. Ask the girls to recall how they have felt when around someone who was happy and smiling, or showing that they truly cared about them. Then ask them how they have felt when they had to be around someone who was angry or mean, who used crude language or didn't seem to care about those around them. Ask them to think about they type of person Jesus wants us to be, have them write those traits that they see in themselves on the other side of their paper. Again, make suggestions to each of the girls. Being a good person can make you a beautiful person inside and out.

Review the section of President Hickely's talk on "Be Clean". Share with your girls his words about how we should care for our sacred bodies.

Show the girls the two magazines you brought. Allow them to look through and observe the young women depicted in both. They should compare clothing, hair, make-up, expression and activities, as well as anything else that catches their eye as a difference or appealing feature. Allow them to discuss their opinions on how they can live the standards of the gospel and develop inner and outer beauty while maintaining their "coolness".

Have the girls refer back to their papers of qualities. Now have them add a few things to the bottom of each side that they would like to work on. Encourage them to set goals and think of ways that they can have an appearance and personality that is pleasing to them and Heavenly Father.

End with the video Johnny Lingo and your testimony that each child is a beautiful daughter of God. He has given each one of us special qualities that can help us grow to be wonderful people.

Activity:

Materials Needed:

* A wide variety of craft materials: buttons, sequins, pipe cleaners, yarn, beans, rocks, craft foam, etc.
* Glue
* Scissors
* Markers
* Large, sturdy paper plates like Chinette®

The girls are to use the plates as their head and face and construct a creative self-portrait.

Use this lesson to reinforce:

* *Gospel Standards*
* *Faith in God*, developing talents
* *Family Home Evening Resource Book*, lesson 5
* *Primary 2*, lesson 3
* *Young Women 1*, lessons 5 and 6
* *Young Women 2*, lesson 47

Special Note: This activity easily lends itself to a "Mother-Daughter All Nighter" (none dare call it a sleep-over!). Have make-overs and manicures, hold a fashion show, and share a good movie about a girl becoming something wonderful (try The Princess Diaries—Walt Disney Studios, Little Women—Columbia Pictures, Anne of Green Gables-Sulliyan Entertainment, or My Fair Lady—MGM studios). You can craft cow printed t-shirts stating "I'm an 8 cow girl" or crowns for princesses in training.

The following books are recommended as excellent sources of girl-friendly advice on becoming a young woman while being true to your self.

* *Princess Lessons* by Meg Cabot
* *The Care and Keeping of You* from American Girls Library
* *Beautiful Girlhood* by Karen Andreola
* *Secret Keeper: The Delicate Power of Modesty* by Dannah Gresh
* *Growing Up* by Brad Wilcox
* *Talking about Growing Up: Real Life Advice from Girls Like You* from Girls World Publications
* *Growing Little Women: Capturing Teaching Moments with Your Daughter* by Donna J. Miller
* *Growing Strong Daughters: Encouraging Girls to Become All They Need to Be* by Lisa Graham McMinn

Seventeen
Building Prayers that Reach to Heaven

Scripture: "Then shall ye call upon me, and ye shall go and pray unto me, and I will hearken unto you. And ye shall seek me, and find me, when ye shall search for me with all your heart."

—Jeremiah 29:12-13

Song: "I Pray in Faith," *Children's Songbook*, pg. 14.

Treat: Celery and peanut butter towers or cake/pretzels/graham crackers and icing towers

Lesson:

Materials Needed:

* At least one chair that is safe for a child to stand on
* Book of Mormon for each child
* Chalk and chalkboard or Marker and poster board
* 4 individual word strips reading: Opening, giving thanks, asking, closure
* Television and video player
* Video of The First Vision: either *Moments from Church History Six Part Videocassette* (15 minutes) or *Doctrine and Covenants and Church History Video Presentations* (9 minutes)
* Paper and writing utensils for each child

Have the children take turns reading verses from Alma 31:8-23. When each child takes their turn, have them stand on top of their chair to read. After all the verses are completed, review the basic story of the Zoramites and the Rameumptom to help them understand what they have read.

Ask the children to share their feelings about the Zoramites' activities, as well as how they felt when it was their turn to stand up and read. Help them understand the Zoramites' motivation for saying their prayers in that manner, and the misunderstandings they had about to whom they were praying and why.

Next share the video of the first vision. Ask the children to compare the two methods of prayer. How were their feelings different when watching the video from when they were reading from their chairs? Ask for their suggestions of when, where and why it is appropriate to pray. Write their answers down on the left-hand side of the chalkboard or poster.

On the right side of the board, draw a ladder with four rungs.

Explain to the children that we don't need real towers or ladders for God to hear us, but we do need to understand whom we're talking to and how to talk to Him. When we understand these things, it is like we are climbing a ladder that brings us closer to Heavenly Father. When we pray because we really do want to talk to our loving Heavenly Father, then the Holy Spirit can be there with us. Those special, warm, and good feelings we experience during our most sincere prayers is Heavenly Father's way of letting us know He is listening and loves us very much.

The ladder is always the same. Each rung is firmly placed to help us keep track of our thoughts and be closer to Heavenly Father as we pray. There is an exact form we should use when we say our prayers. Have the children randomly draw out the prepared word strips and place them in order on the rungs of the ladder. As each item is placed let the children voice their ideas on what each thing means. Then help them to think further about what they can do to improve each of these areas.

Remind them that part of opening their prayers is showing reverence and respect for Heavenly Father through our mannerisms and how we chose to address Him. Remind them that we fold our arms, bow our heads, close our eyes, and sometimes kneel in order to ready ourselves for prayer and show respect. We chose a simple but respectful way to address Heavenly Father that helps us remember who we are talking to and how much we love Him. Demonstrate that there is also a language of reverence that we should continue to use during our prayers. Have the children open their scriptures and find the words that are used as pronouns. Challenge the children to try and remember to use Thee, Thou, and Thine when talking to Heavenly Father during their prayers.

Help the children brainstorm things that can be included in thegiving thanks and asking sections of a prayer. Have the children try two exercises. For the first, allow one minute in which to write down everything that they can think of that happened to them that day that they can be thankful for. Share the lists. Next, time them for another minute where they must be as quiet as possible and listen. They are to list on their papers every sound that they heard during that time. Once again have them share their lists. Help the children understand that these are two important parts of saying good prayers. If we think before we pray, our prayers will come more from our hearts than just from our mouths (see Moroni 7:9).

If we learn to listen quietly as we pray it is easier for us to feel the spirit. Compare listening for answers during our prayers to asking their school teachers for help, then walking away before their teacher could help them. When we pray with our hearts we know Heavenly Father is listening and wants to tell us how much we are loved.

Review the proper form for closing a prayer, by using the name of Jesus Christ, thereby recognizing His role as our Savior and Mediator. Explain that as part of the atonement Christ came to understand our hopes and struggles. He willingly carries our prayers to Heavenly Father.

Activity:

Materials Needed:

* Chutes and Ladders® game
* Additional assorted game pieces for individual play, or form the children into teams

Play Chutes and Ladders® with the following variation. The children must review one thing they learned about prayer from the lesson before they can move. They can save themselves from backsliding by giving an example of a common mistake made when offering prayers.

Or if you wish, devise a set of questions to draw from that must be answered before they can complete a move. If a question is answered wrongly they must go down the nearest slide and "repent" until their next turn.

When they reach the top of the game board, their prayers have made it to heaven; make sure everyone completes the game so no one feels discouraged.

Use this lesson to reinforce:

* *My Gospel Standards*
* *Faith in God*, general requirements and learning and living the gospel
* Cub Scouts, Wolf, Bear and Webelos religious requirements
* *Family Home Evening Resource Book*, lesson 7
* *Primary 4*, lesson 21
* *Aaronic Priesthood 3*, lesson 18
* *Young Women 1*, lesson 24

Eighteen
The Family Proclamation

Scripture: "Organize yourselves; prepare every needful thing; and establish a house, even a house of prayer, a house of fasting, a house of faith, a house of learning, a house of glory, a house of order, a house of God."

—D&C 88:119

Song: "Families Can Be Together Forever," *Children's Songbook*, pg. 188.

Treat: Doughnuts or other round treat

Lesson:

Materials Needed:

* Copies of "The Family Proclamation" for each child
* Large circle cut out of construction paper
* Large rubber band
* Picture of a traditional family
* Index cards or slips of paper with the situations listed below written on them
* Scissors

Show the children the cut out circle and ask them to describe everything that they can about it. Next, show the rubber band and ask them to compare the two objects. What can they tell you about the band, how is the same or different from the paper? Now show the picture of a family. Ask the children if the people in the picture have anything in common with the circle and the rubber band. Allow them to voice their thoughts and opinions.

The family is an important part of Heavenly Father's plan for us. A circle is often used to represent something that is infinite, continuous or eternal. That is the way Heavenly Father intends our families to be. Ask them to tell you about how a family can become an eternal unit.

Use your scissors to cut out a section of the paper circle. Is the circle still whole? What is missing or wrong? Are all families on earth whole? What can be missing or go wrong? Allow answer freely. Remind the children that Heavenly Father understands that not all of our families will look or work in exactly the same way, but we have a responsibility to try our best to have a happy family and live the gospel. If we do these things, Heavenly Father will make up the difference.

Show the children the rubber band again. A family that has been sealed in the temple has tried to make sure their circle is complete, but it still must work and change and grow.

Stretch the rubber band so that it expands. The more we work to be like Jesus and love and care for each member of our family our circle grows and so does our happiness.

Every member of a family shares the responsibility for the unit's happiness. Every member plays an important roll and has unique things to share with the others.

Show the children the family proclamations. Share with them that to help us understand what God expects of us as members of a family and his children this statement was published. Many people today have forgotten how important a family is. Have the children help you take turns reading the proclamation. Explain any words that appear difficult for them. Then review, once again, the middle of the seventh paragraph.

"Happiness in family life is most likely to be achieved when founded upon the teachings of the Lord Jesus Christ. Successful marriages and families are established and maintained on principles of faith, prayer, repentance, forgiveness, respect, love compassion, work, and wholesome recreational activities." (The Family: A Proclamation To The World, 1995)

Have the children break into pairs and role-play some of the situations listed here, or any others you feel prompted to use.

* A mother and daughter disagree about when the daughter should come home from a party.
* A girl's boyfriend says he wants to marry her, but he doesn't want a temple wedding. He says that he wants her to have a big, fancy wedding where she can feel special. Besides, they can always go to the temple later.
* A family must decide whether to go to church on Sunday or begin their vacation a day early.
* Your little brother wants to play with you and your friend, but he's really a pain and never plays right.
* A pair of sisters has been fighting. Each is sure that they are right and the other is being mean and unfair.
* Your brother put a dent in dad's car but he isn't going to tell. He says your dad will never notice, or will just think he did it himself.
* Your mother is sick, but you are hungry and can't find anything you want to eat.

Emphasize the importance of working together to make a family happy and successful. Ask the children to brainstorm some of the things they can do in their own homes to help things be more like Heavenly Father would want them to be.

Activity:

Materials Needed:

* Pink and Red construction paper
* Scissors
* Yarn
* Hole punch
* Tape
* Writing utensils

Help the children draw and cut out 5 large hearts each. Have the children write something on each heart that they can do to help strengthen their family. Then, have the children punch two holes in the top of each heart and string them onto a strand of yarn. Leave a little space between each heart. They can secure them in place with a piece of tape over the yarn on the back of each heart.

Encourage them to take their hearts home and hang them up some place that will remind them of their goals.

Use this lesson to reinforce:

* *My Gospel Standards*
* *Faith in God*, general requirements, developing talents, and preparing for Young Women's and the Priesthood
* Cub Scouts Wolf, Bear and Webelos religious requirements, also Wolf Elective 2a
* *Family Home Evening Resource Book*, lessons 17 and 21 and "The Family: A Proclamation To The World"
* *For the Strength of Youth*
* *Young Women Personal Progress*
* *D&C and Church History Gospel Doctrine Manual*, lesson 45

Nineteen
Tithing Builds the Kingdom

Scripture: "Behold, this is the tithing and the sacrifice which I, the Lord, require at their hands, that there may be a house built unto me for the salvation of Zion."

—D&C 97:12

Song: "I Want to Give the Lord My Tenth," *Children's Songbook*, pg. 150.

Treat: Gingersnaps—"penny cookies"

Lesson:

Materials Needed:

* Chalkboard and chalk or dry-erase board and marker
* 6 large brown paper circles can be traced from a #10 can
* Marker
* Tape

Before the lesson, list these questions individually on your circles: What is it, Why pay it, Who has to pay it, How much should I pay, What happens when the bishop gets it, and Do I get anything back.

Write "tithing" on the top of your board. Then place your penny circles, in the order listed above, down the left side of the board. Tell the children that you are going to discuss tithing tonight and answer these questions. Ask the children each question and list their answers by each appropriate circle, add any items they may have missed when they have exhausted all their own answers. A list of appropriate answers is included at the bottom of this lesson.

Close this lesson with your own testimony of tithing.

This lesson is meant to be a brief over-view, not involved and detailed, as the accompanying activity will take the majority of the time. The object is to give the children a concrete example of what their tithing money, however small, can help to accomplish. It also provides a sense of satisfaction and accomplishment to see their labors rewarded.

The following points should be included in your discussion:

* Tithing is ten percent of all your income. Show the children how to "hop" the decimal point to the left one number place to make 10% of the whole number and round up the change to get the amount of their tithing for any amount of money.
* Tithing is a way we can show gratitude for the blessings Heavenly Father gives us.

* Paying tithing is a test of faith and a commandment.
* Paying a full tithing is a requirement for getting a temple recommend.
* If we pay our tithing, Heavenly Father will give us even more blessings.
* We pay our tithing to our bishop or branch president. They send the money to the headquarters of the church.
* The First Presidency, Quorum of the Twelve Apostles, and Presiding Bishopric prayerfully determine where the money should be used.
* Tithing money usually pays for things like the welfare program, building temples and church buildings and maintaining our buildings, sometimes even for education needs. It also supports missionaries and family history programs.

Activity:

Materials Needed:

* 400 piece Coinstruction® kit (can be found at educational or hobby stores, approximate cost $15)
* 138 Pennies (divide total amount by number of children in your group and ask each child to try and contribute at least that amount)
* Several copies of the instructions
* Consider building a display platform, modeling the temple grounds, for your penny temple and presenting the entire finished project as a gift to your bishop or branch president.
* If you live in an area of great financial difficulty, make this a long term project where children gradually bring in their pennies and other small change over the year, use the pennies in the construction and any other change to help pay for the kit.

Tell the children that just as Heavenly Father has asked us to pay tithing so that he can bless us with things we need, you have asked them to bring something with them to help build a special project. Commend the children for their efforts in obeying and ask them if they would like to see what their pennies could build.

Use the instructions and diagram provided to construct a temple from the children's pennies.

Pass out the copies of the instructions so that everyone has a set that they can refer to, set out the joiner pieces and assign children to different parts of the temple to try and construct it. Help the children as needed but allow them to experiment and problem-solve for themselves.

Use this lesson to reinforce:

* *My Gospel Standards*
* *Faith in God*, general requirements and developing talents
* Cub Scouts Wolf, Bear and Webelos religious requirements, also Wolf Elective 5g and Bear Achievement 21a and b
* *Family Home Evening Resource Book*, lesson idea "tithing"
* *Primary 2*, lesson 33
* *Primary 3*, lesson 42
* *Primary 5*, lesson 45

* *Primary 6*, lesson 44
* *Primary 7*, lesson 24
* *Aaronic Priesthood 1*, lesson 20
* *Aaronic Priesthood 2*, lesson 16
* *D&C and Church History Gospel Doctrine Manual*, lesson 17
* *Gospel Principles*, chapter 32

Temple Instructions

Materials Needed:

* Roof Top—32 coins, 20 straight two-way connectors, 32 three-way connectors
* Rear Wall—24 coins, 8 right angle connectors, 37 straight two-way connectors
* Front Wall—24 coins, 8 right angle connectors, 31 straight two-way connectors, 6 three-way connectors
* Left Side—12 coins, 10 right angle connectors, 17 straight two-way connectors
* Right Side—12 coins, 10 right angle connectors, 17 straight two-way connectors
* Front Entrance—12 coins, 12 straight two-way connectors, 4 right angle connectors
* Spire—22 coins, 4 three-way connectors, 4 right angle connectors, 6 four-way connectors, 12 straight two-way connectors

1. Separate out the needed materials for each section.
2. Construct each piece as illustrated first.
3. After all the pieces have been assembled according to the diagram, join the sides and top of the front entrance.
4. Attach the entrance to the open connectors on the front wall.
5. Join front, sides and back walls to form a rectangle.
6. Place the roof upside down on your work surface
7. Flip walls upside down so the open connectors are facing down.
8. Join roof onto walls using the work surface for stability.
9. Turn back right side up, so that roof is on top of the building.
10. Gently squeeze the form together to settle all the pieces into place and improve stability.
11. Join the sections of the spire together.
12. Place one hand under the roof section for support.
13. Attach the spire to the open connectors on the roof.

Hints: The connectors are easier to work with if they have been previously fitted with a coin. Note that you can load coins directly from the front of the connector or slide them in from the sides when fitting into tight spaces.

Parts Identifier

Penny (laid flat)

Penny (on edge)

4-way Connector

3-way Connector

2-way Connector (right angle)

2-way Connector (straight)

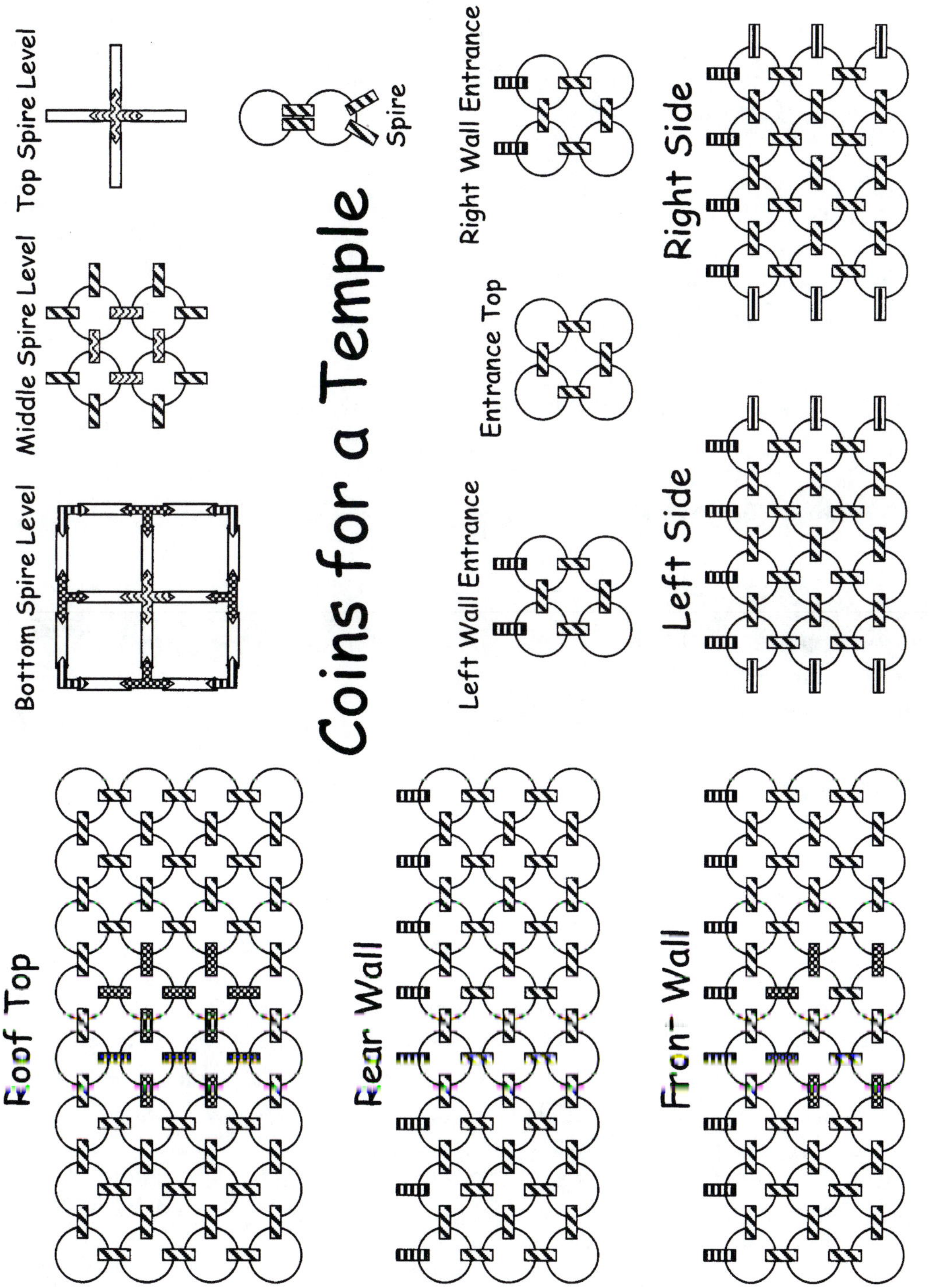
Coins for a Temple
Top Spire Level
Middle Spire Level
Bottom Spire Level
Spire
Right Wall Entrance
Entrance Top
Left Wall Entrance
Right Side
Left Side
Roof Top
Rear Wall
Front Wall

Twenty
The Gift of the Holy Ghost

Scripture: "Yea, behold, I will tell you in your mind and in your heart, by the Holy Ghost, which shall come upon you and which shall dwell in your heart. Now, behold, this is the spirit of revelation; behold, this is the spirit by which Moses brought the children of Israel through the Red Sea on dry ground."

—D&C 8:2-3

Song: "The Still Small Voice," *Children's Songbook*, pg. 106.

Treat: Heart shaped cookies with messages from the Holy Ghost written on them in the fashion of candy conversation hearts

Lesson:

Materials Needed:

* A large comforter or quilt
* Rocking chair or other comfortable chair
* Copy of the scriptures for each child
* Gospel art picture #107 "Moses and the Burning Bush"

Be familiar with the story of Moses found in Exodus 3:1-5.

Greet the children outside of the classroom and ask them to please remove their shoes and leave them outside before entering.

Start by asking the children to describe everything that they know about the Holy Ghost and his purpose in each of our lives.

Ask one of the children to sit down in the rocking chair, wrap up in your quilt, and rock quietly for a minute. Ask all of the children to think of a time when they have been scared, nervous or alone and to remember what those feelings were like.

Have the child in the quilt try and share what it feels like to be safe and comfortable. Remind the children to think of how it felt when their feelings of anxiety were relieved; also, have them think of times when they have felt happy and at peace. Have a few of them try to share how they felt at those times.

Compare the feelings of comfort and peace during each experience. Help them realize that these feelings are from the Holy Ghost. Read John 14:16-17 with the children. Have them mark these verses with a colored pencil.

Feelings are not always easy to understand or recognize. Understanding how the Holy Ghost works will help us to identify what it feels like when the spirit is with us. As we become more aware of these feelings, we will feel the presence of the spirit with us more often. He can help us in many ways. Read 2 Nephi 32:5 and Moroni 10:5 and mark the verses with the children. The Holy Ghost is there to lead, teach and comfort us, and show us how to become more like Jesus Christ. It is through His influence that we gain our testimonies of Jesus Christ.

Remind the children that you had them take off their shoes when they entered the room. Show them the picture of Moses and share the story depicted. Help them realize that Moses had to prepare himself to hear the message of the Lord by removing something of himself that represented the world. This was his shoes. The more we practice removing worldly things from our lives and begin looking towards those things that we have been asked to do, the more we will be able to have the spirit as our companion.

Allow the children to suggest ways that they can remove the world and draw closer to the Spirit so He can dwell with us. These should include: scripture study, prayer, attending our meetings, living the word of wisdom and keeping what we read, watch and listen to appropriate.

Activity:

Materials Needed:

* Copies of the symbols and scripture references for each child
* Several sheets of tissue paper
* Colored pencils
* Each child's personal scriptures. If some children do not have their own scriptures try to arrange for them to have a set of their own before this activity or give them a special three ring binder to collect scripture phrases in. They can trace and copy the scripture onto plain copier paper and hole-punch them for storage in their notebook.

Show the children that they will be looking up scriptures about the Holy Ghost and tracing in the corresponding picture to remind them what the scripture is about. Have them practice using a light touch to trace and color their pictures on tissue paper. Remind them not to press to hard or color darkly or they will tear their pages or not be able to read the words underneath. As they color, read and discuss with them what each of the scriptures means and represents.

Use this lesson to reinforce:

* *My Gospel Standards*
* *Faith In God*, learning and living the gospel
* Cub Scouts Wolf, Bear and Webelos religious requirements
* *Family Home Evening Resource Book*, lesson 15
* *Primary 1*, lesson 7
* *Primary 2*, lesson 13
* *Primary 3*, lesson 12
* *Primary 7*, lesson 36
* *Gospel Principles*, chapters 7 and 21
* *Aaronic Priesthood 1*, lesson 6
* *Aaronic Priesthood 2*, lesson 4
* *Aaronic Priesthood 3*, lesson 17
* *Young Women 1*, lesson 4

John 15:26

2 Nephi 31:17

D&C 11:13
Note: There are two verses on this page, leave room for both.

Matthew 12:18

Comforter

Moroni 8:26

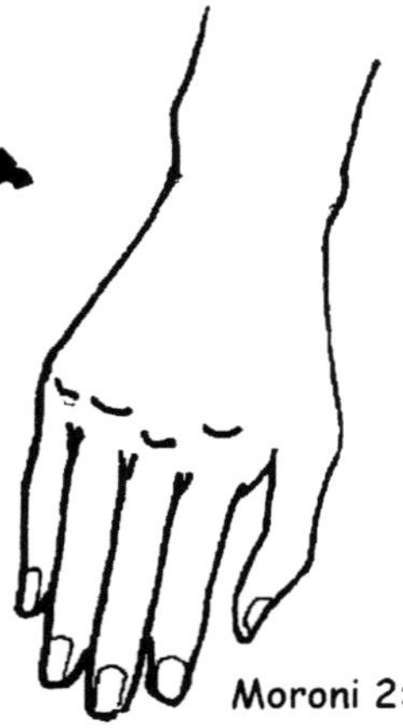

Moroni 2:1-3

1 Nephi 11:27

2 Nephi 33:1

D&C 11:12
Note: there are two verses on this page, leave room for both

2 Peter 1:21

Exodus 31:3

D&C 130:22

John 14:26

Twenty-one
The Sacrament is for Me

Scripture: "And as they were eating, Jesus took bread, and blessed it, and brake it, and gave it to the disciples, and said, Take, eat; this is my body. And he took the cup, and gave thanks, and gave it to them, saying Drink ye all of it; For this is my blood of the new testament, which is shed for many for the remission of sins."

—Matthew 26:26-28

Song: "Before I Take the Sacrament," *Children's Songbook*, pg. 73.

Treat: Grapes, Cheese in block form, homemade bread (or pita bread) and white grape juice

Note: This activity requires a longer block of time; consider using this as a special two hour Saturday or summer activity.

Lesson:

Materials Needed:

* Copy of the scriptures for each child
* Chalk and Chalkboard
* Large long table that can be lowered to just above the floor
* Simple tablecloth
* Cushions and bean bags for sitting one
* Small tub
* Pitcher of water
* Towel
* Framed picture of Christ
* One chair, preferably wood and low to the ground
* Tape or CD player
* Tape or CD of the hymns, preferably orchestral, or other soft appropriate music
* Small cups for each child
* A napkin for each child, cloth is more appropriate if available

Prepare table with food and cushions. Set the chair, tub, a pitcher of water and a towel off to one side. Place the picture of Christ in a central location where it can be easily seen by all. Play music very softly in the background.

Begin your lesson outside of this room.

Have some children look up Mosiah 18:10, D&C 20:37, D&C 33:11, 3 Nephi 11:33 and D&C 20: 77-79. Read through the above scriptures and write down on the chalkboard the things called out that have to do with our baptism and the covenants we make there. Make a separate list of the things we should remember and promise each time we take the sacrament. Emphasize that when we take the sacrament, it is a time to remember Christ and the promises we have made with Him. In return He continues to be with us and help us be more like Him.

We can help this process by being particularly reverent during the sacrament.

Ask the children to give you some ideas of appropriate behavior during the sacrament. List their ideas on the board. Make sure singing the sacrament song, listening to the prayers and trying to focus on the Savior and how we are trying to be like him are mentioned.

Tell the children that you have prepared an activity to help them focus their thoughts during the sacrament. You will walk them through the events of the first sacrament as the Savior presented it. You will represent the Savior and each of them will play the role of the disciples at the Last Supper.

Take them to the room you have prepared and let them sit around the table and piece at the food laid out for them. Take each child aside individually and wash their feet for them as the Savior did. As you do, quietly talk to them about the things you see in them that are most like the Savior.

When each child has had a chance to experience having their feet washed, share Jesus' words with them as found in John 13:34-35.

Then present a piece of unleavened or homemade bread and share Matthew 26:26. Allow them each to break off and eat a piece of the bread.

Fill their cups with a small bit of grape juice and share Matthew 26:27-28.

Remind them that after this supper, Christ went with his disciples to the garden of Gethsemane where he took upon himself all of our sins and imperfections. He came to know each one of us personally and willingly pronounced us clean through His perfect life. Shortly after this, He was taken to the cross where He died and rose again so that we could have eternal life.

It is these things that we should remember when we are baptized and take the sacrament. Share your testimony with them in closing.

Clear the table for use during your activity.

Activity:

Materials Needed:

* Small photo album for each child
* Variety of 2"x3" pictures of Jesus available at your local LDS bookstores or printed off the internet. Distribution available Article of Faith and Pass-along cards will also work.
* Variety of scrapbook materials
* Glue
* Scissors

Children will create a sacrament scrapbook, this can be used during the sacrament to help them focus on the Savior and the atonement and to help others understand what it means to the child. You might want to invite a member of your ward who is talented at scrap-booking to help the children put theirs together with the pictures and scriptures listed about the Savior.

They should be aloud to put their books together in a manner that is meaningful to them, and copy the scriptures that mean the most to them. Invite them to take their books home and share what they have learned about the sacrament and the covenants they have made with their families in their next family home evening.

The Scriptures used in the lesson can be used as well as any of the following. You might choose to have typed copies of some of the scriptures available for the children to simply cut out and secure into their books and decorate, rather than have them spend their time individually writing the scriptures. This can be discouraging for some children.

* Luke 18:16-17
* John 3:16
* John 10:27
* John 11:25
* Hebrews 4:15
* Mosiah 2:21
* Mosiah 4:9
* Mosiah 10:4
* 3 Nephi 27:27

Use this lesson to reinforce:
* *My Gospel Standards*
* *Faith in God*, general requirements
* "Cub Scouts" Wolf, Bear and Webelos religious requirements
* *Family Home Evening Resource Book*, lesson 14
* *Primary 1*, lesson 40 and 42
* *Primary 3*, lessons 32, 33 and 40
* *Primary 5*, lesson 12
* *Primary 6*, lesson 5
* *Gospel Principles*, chapter 23
* *New Testament Gospel Doctrine Manual*, lesson 23
* *D&C and Church History Gospel Doctrine Manual*, lesson 16
* *Aaronic Priesthood 1*, lesson 35
* *Aaronic Priesthood 3*, lesson 22
* *Young Women 1*, lesson 17
* *Young Women 2*, lesson 26

Index

About the Author

Alison Palmer is a life-long member of the Church. Born in Mesa, Arizona, she grew up in West Virginia and graduated from Marshall University with a Bachelors degree in Nursing. Alison stopped practicing nursing after several years to raise and home school her children.

Over the years, Alison has held many callings in the church, including several that have helped develop her great love for the Primary children. She has served as nursery leader, pianist, chorister, teacher, den leader and Primary President. She has also been spotted teaching Sunday School, serving as a teacher or leader in Relief Society and occasionally braving girl's camp.

Writing is Alison's favorite pastime, but you can also find her lost within the pages of a good book, sewing, cooking, attending the temple, taking long walks or playing with her family. Alison's greatest accomplishments come from the dynamic rewards of raising children who are trying to live righteously.

The Palmers currently reside in Grand Blanc, Michigan.